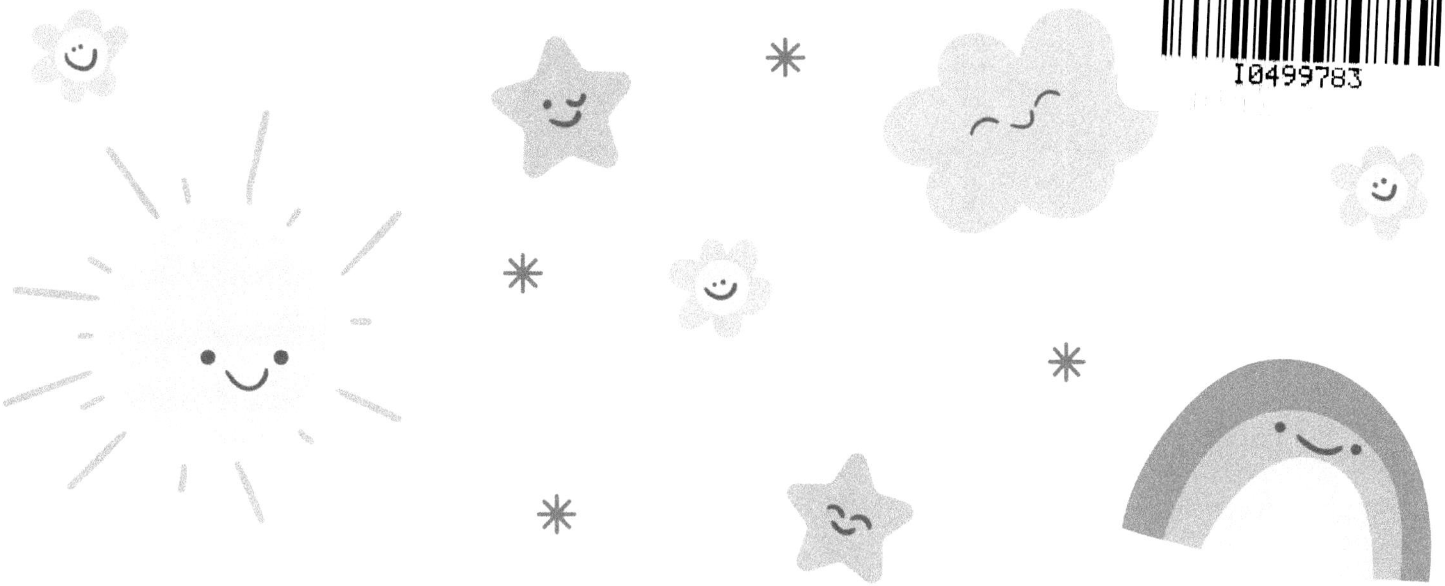

This Books Belongs To.........

....

....

....

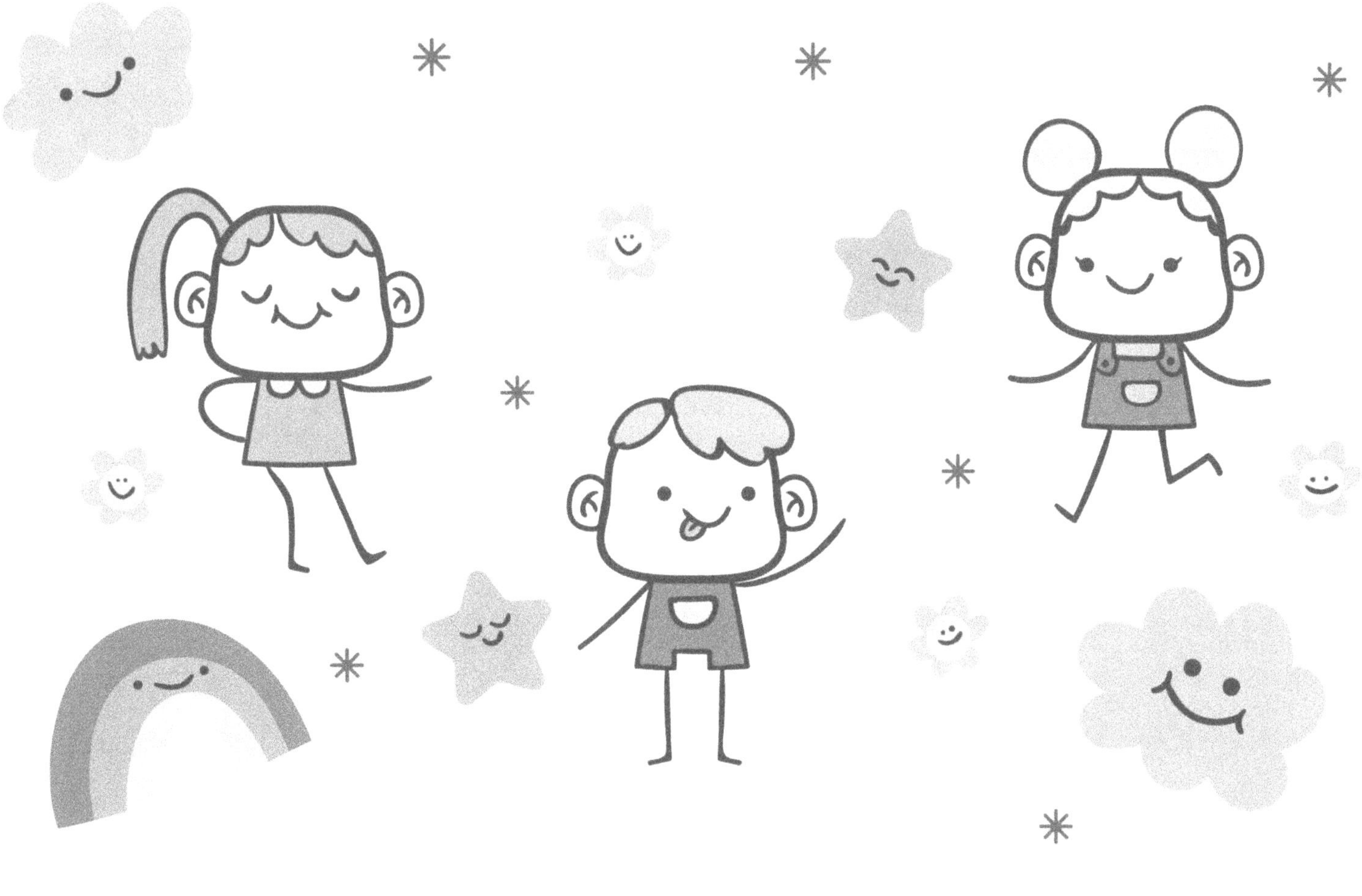

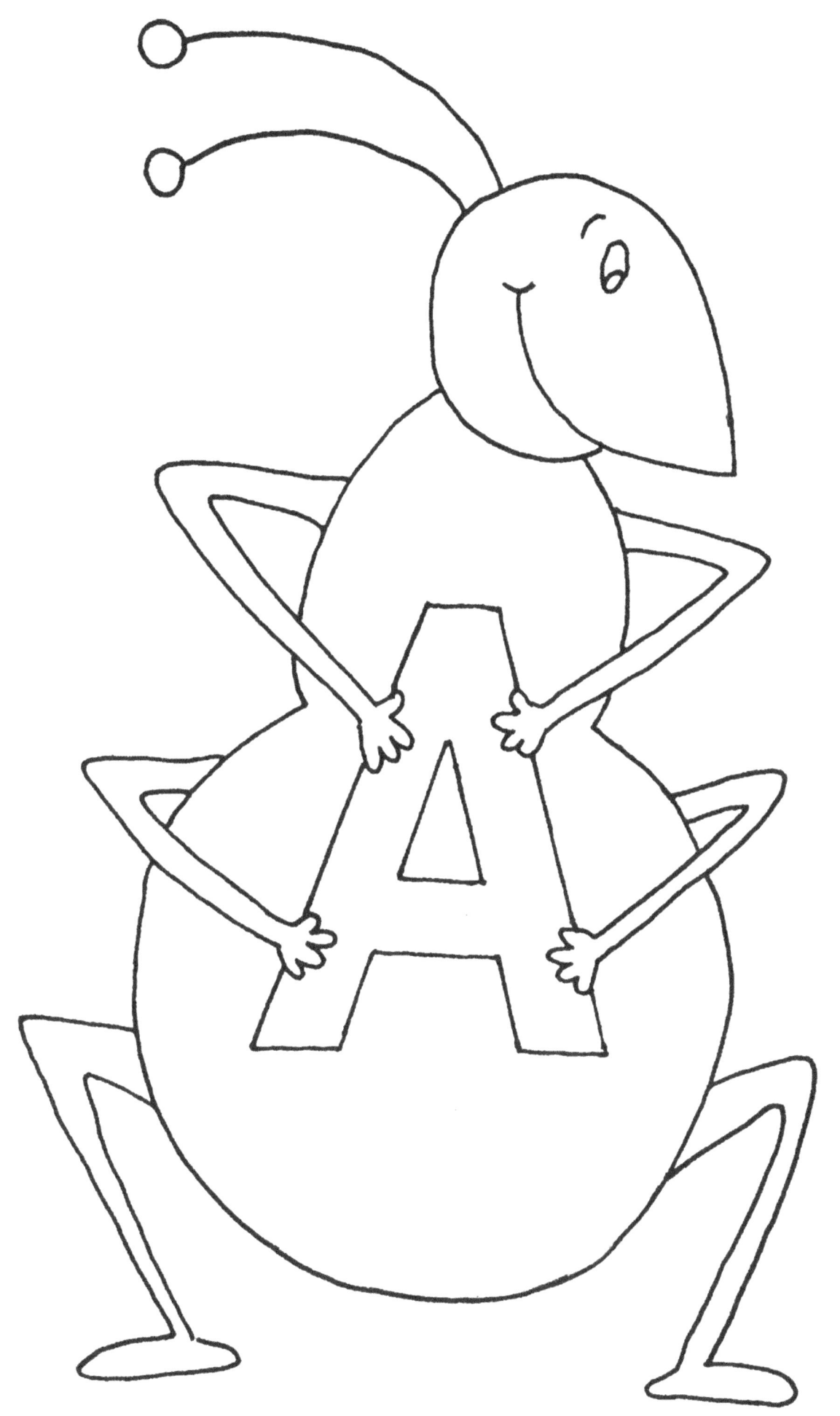

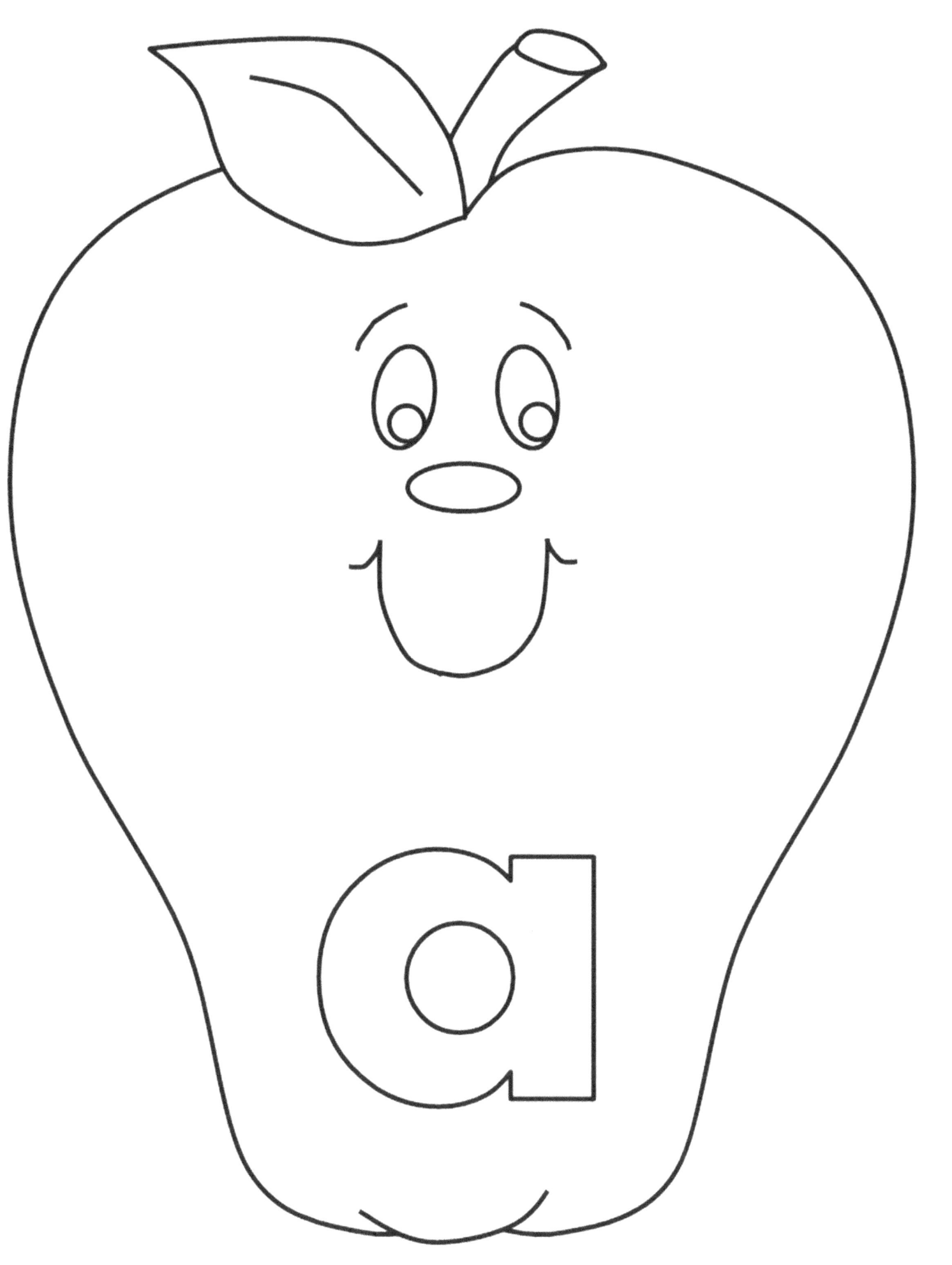

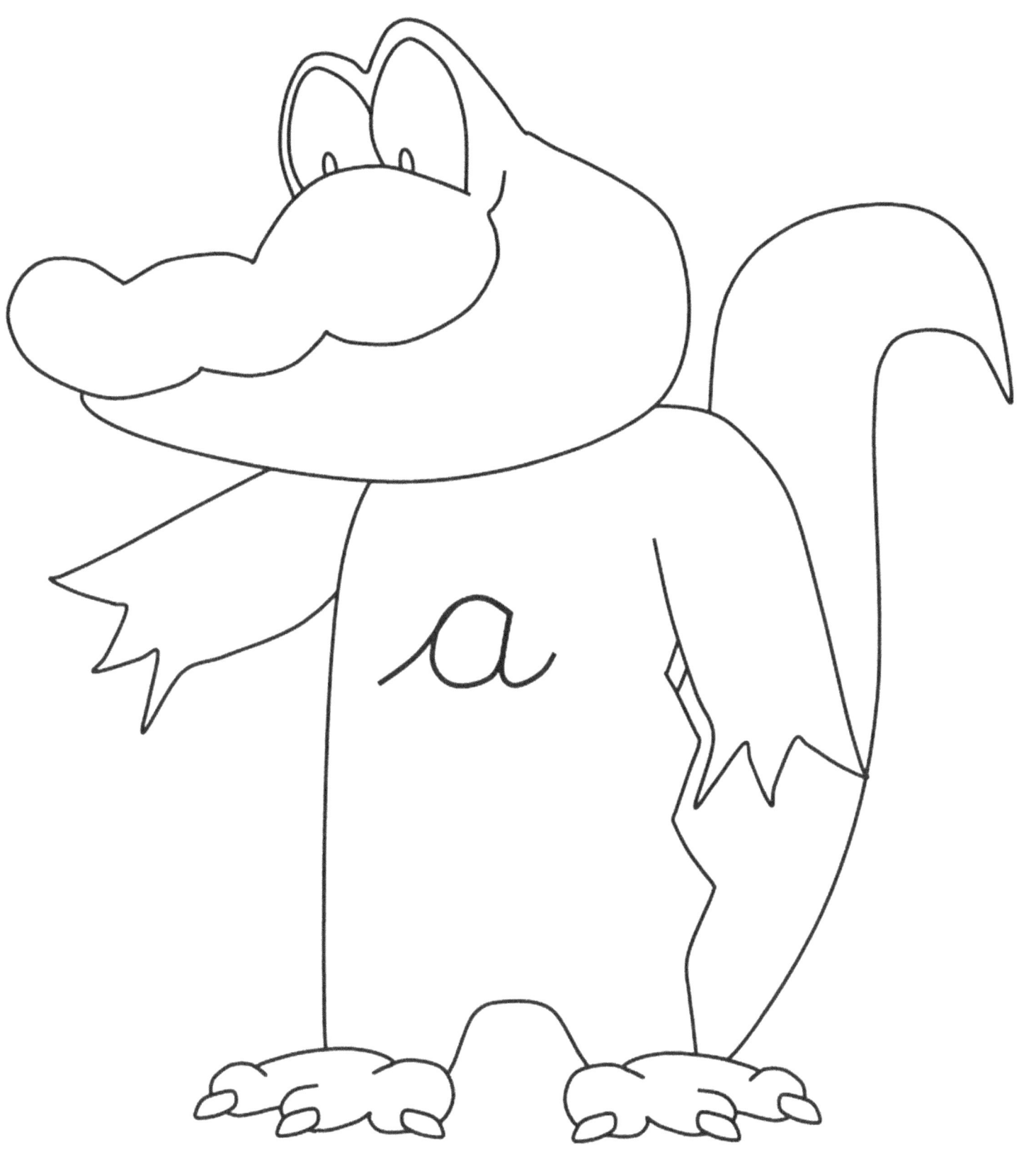

Trace the steps for making the letter a on the following line.

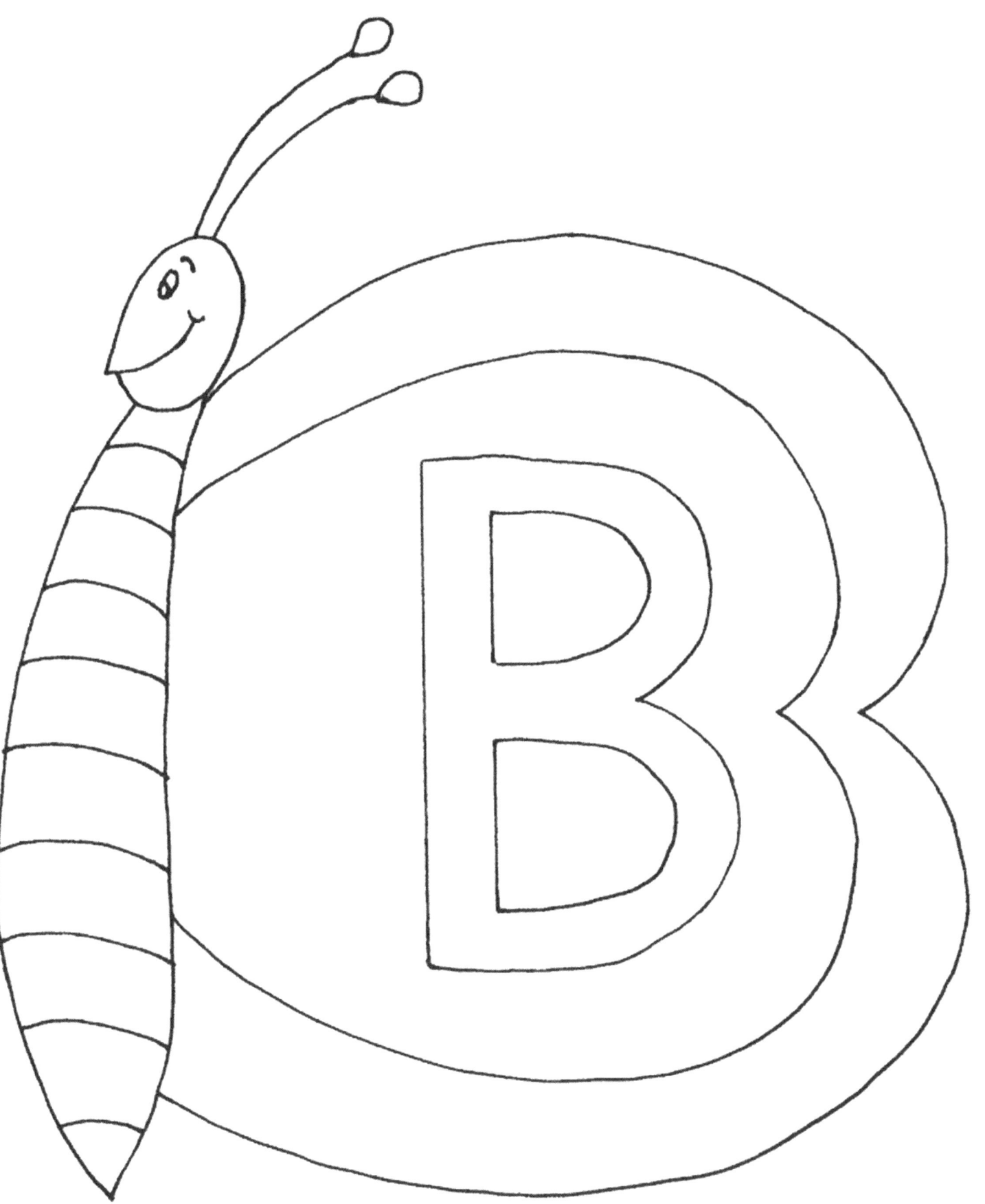

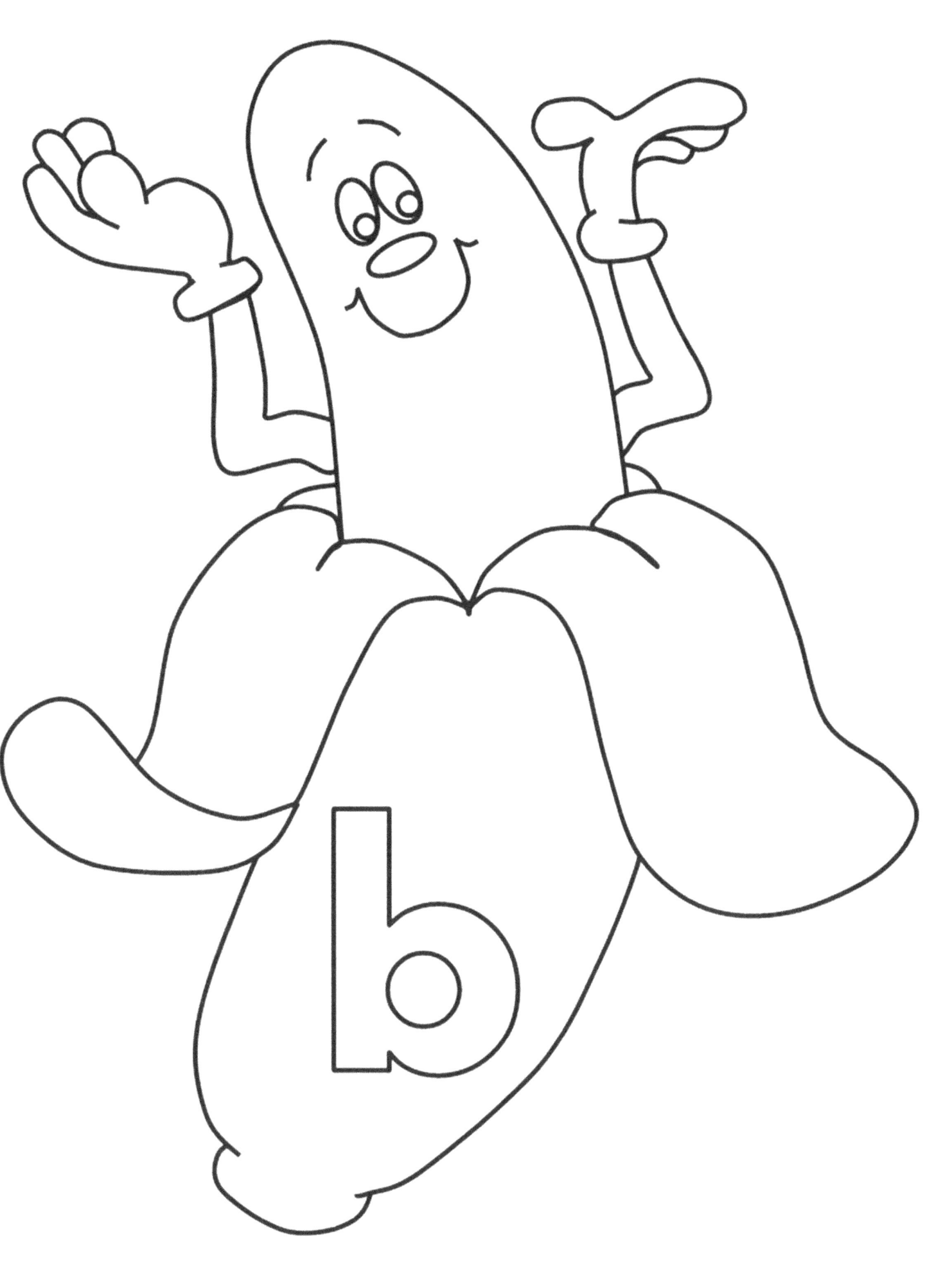

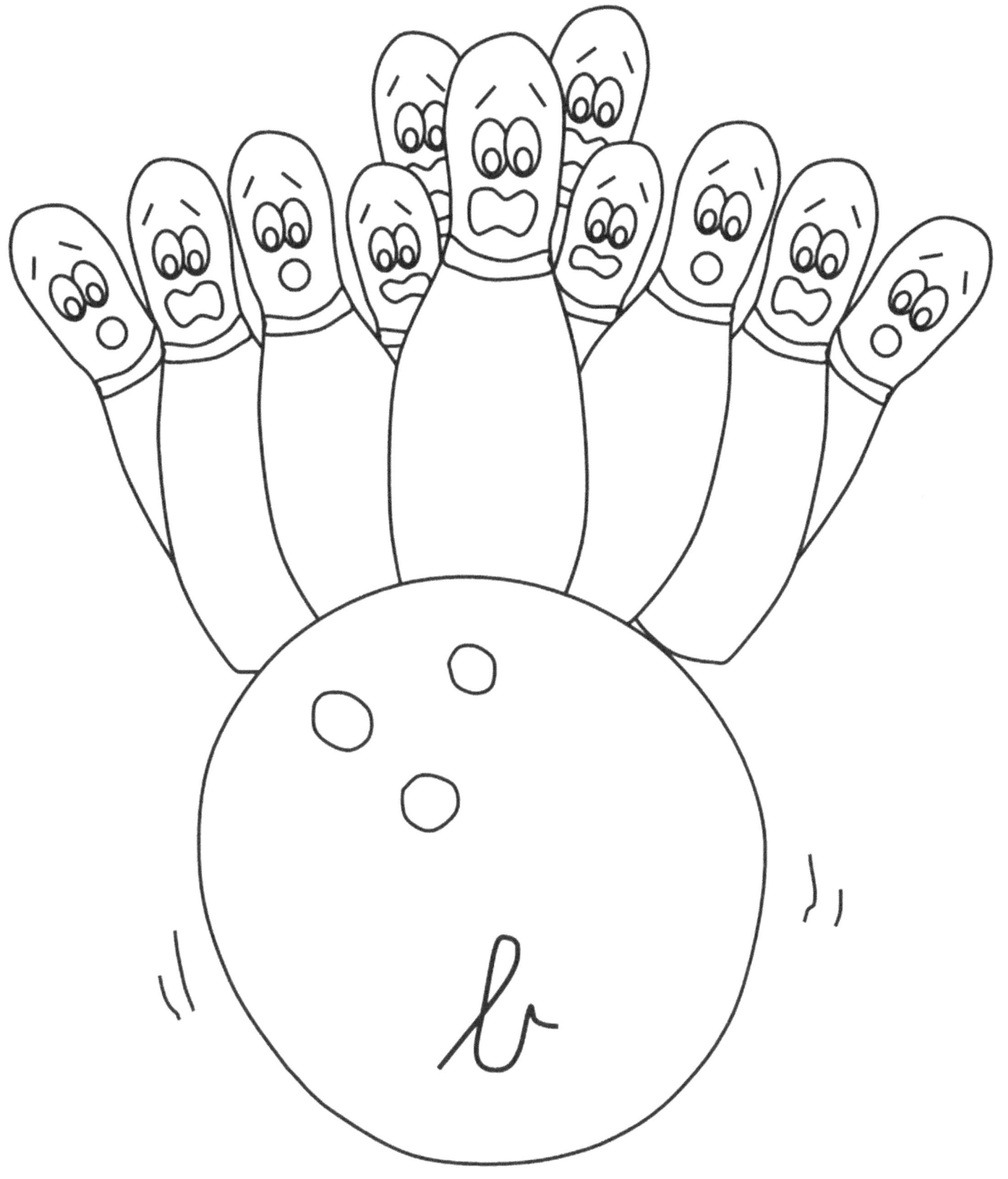

Trace the steps for making the letter b on the following line.

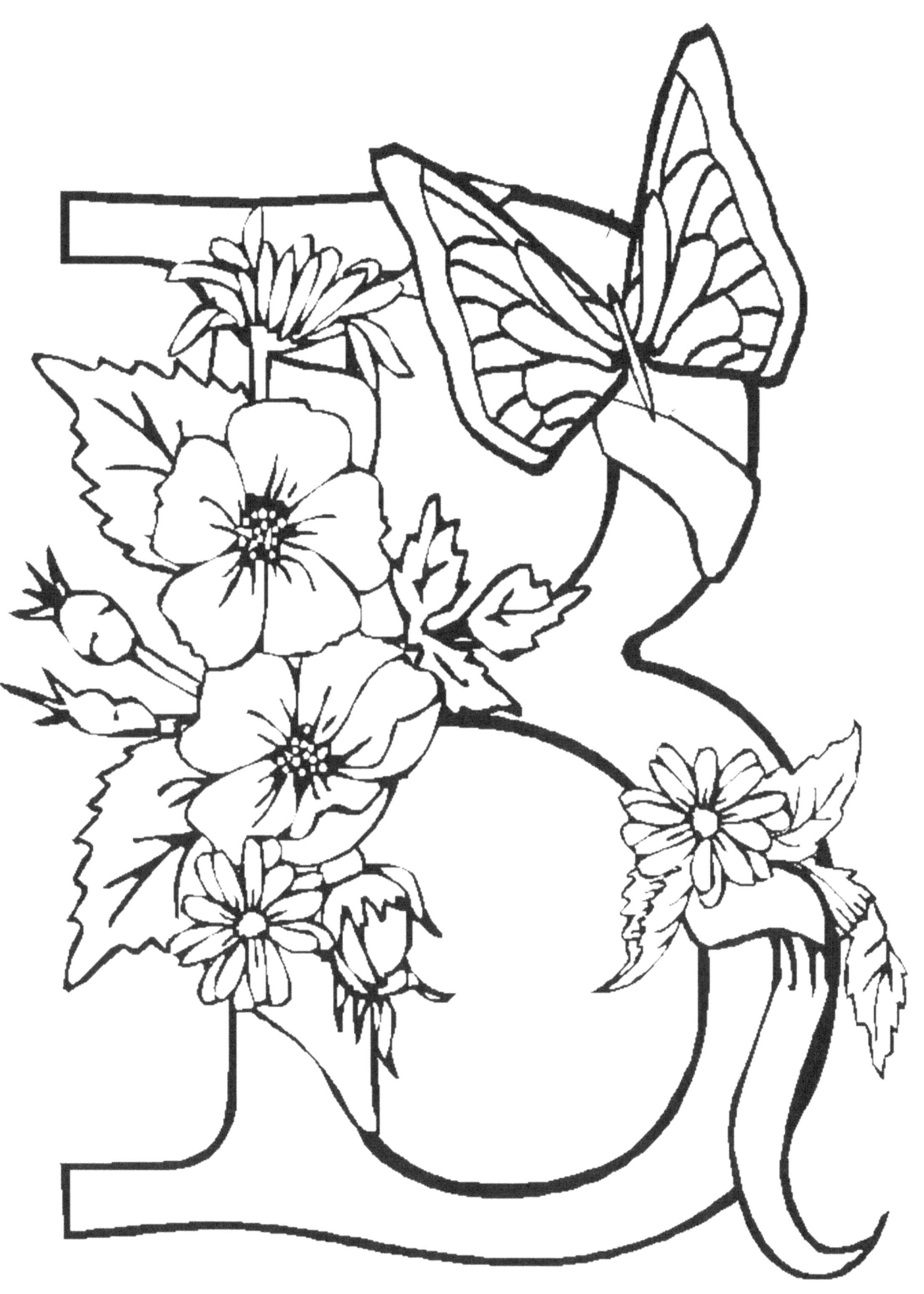

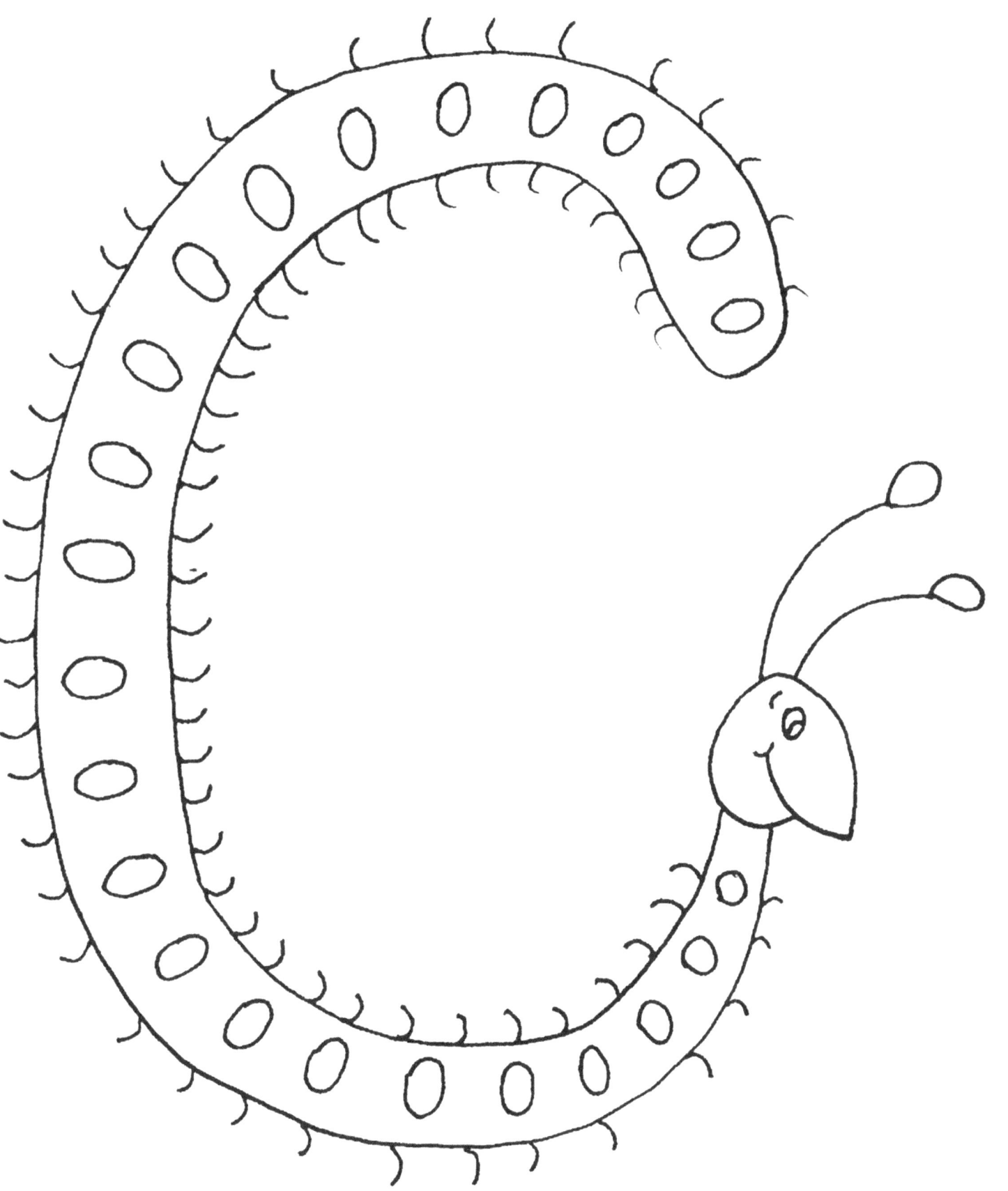

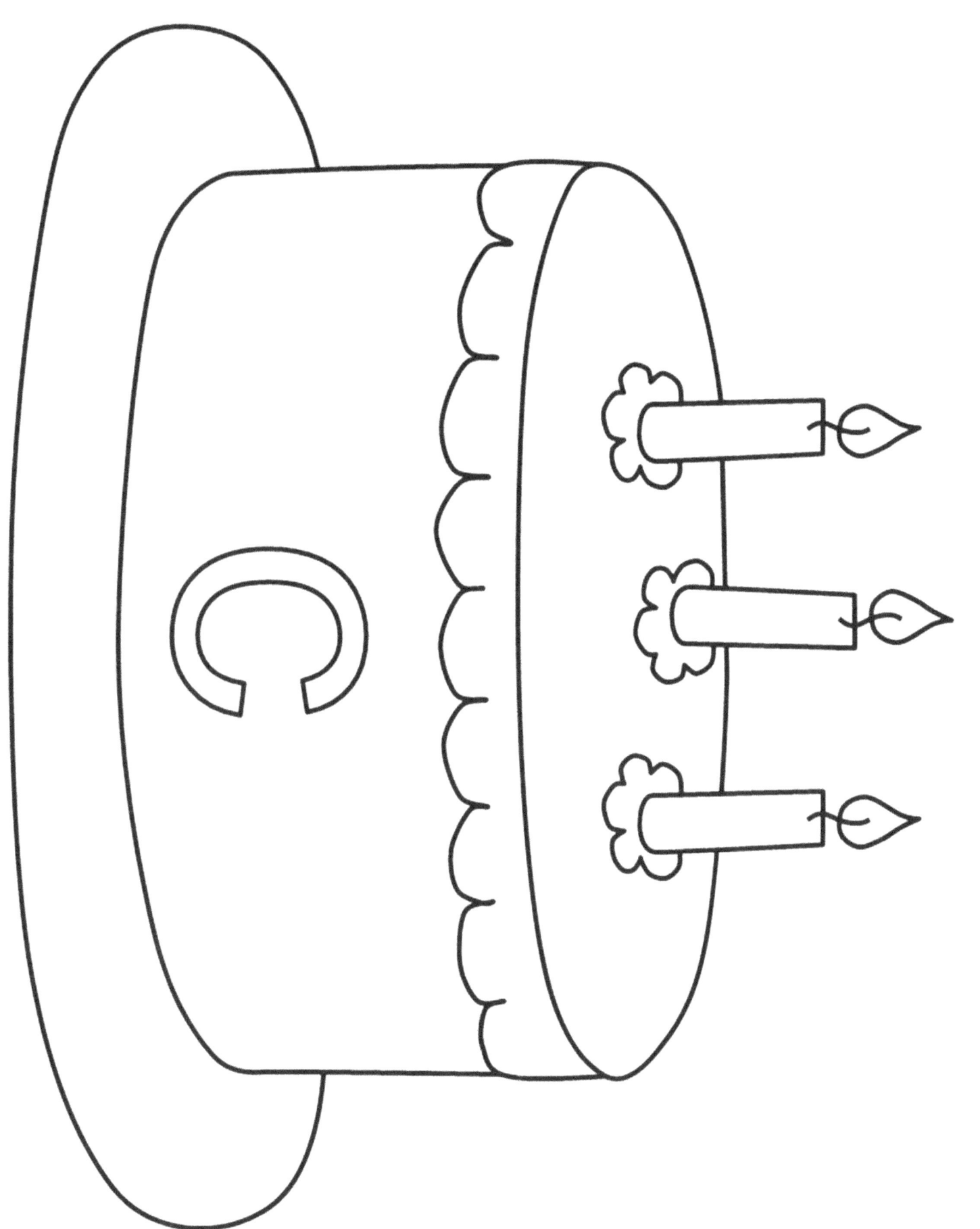

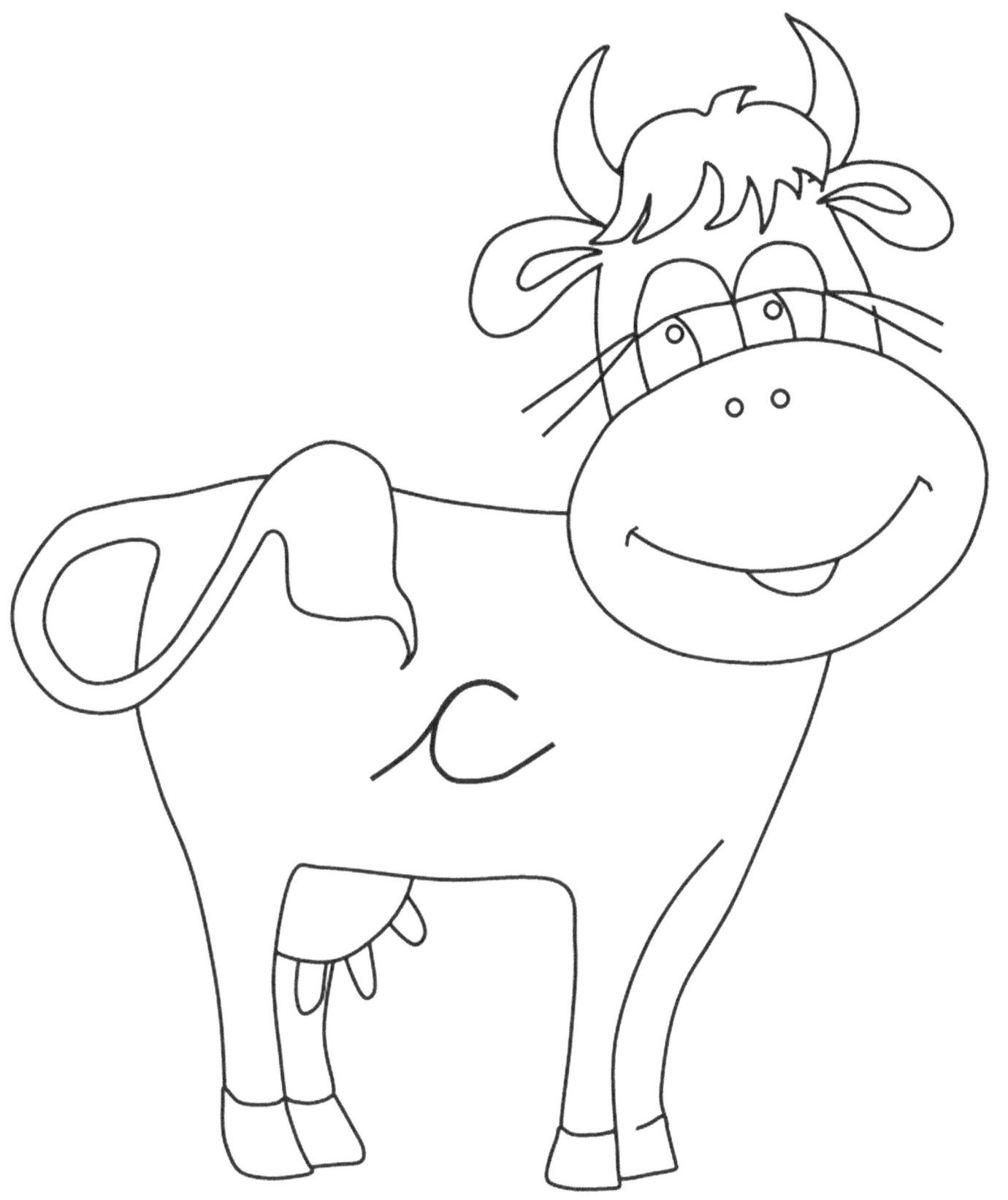

Trace the steps for making the letter c on the following line.

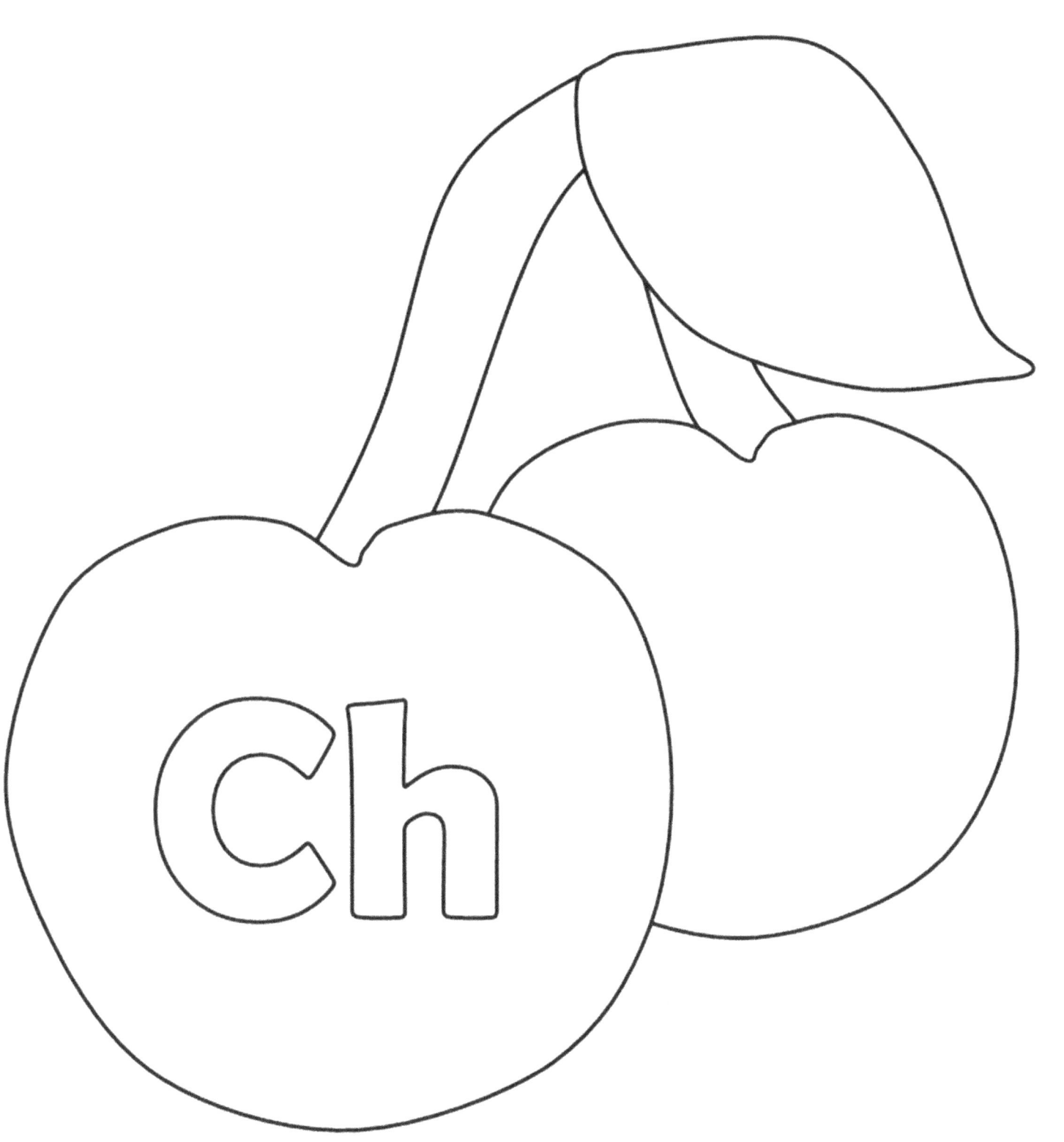

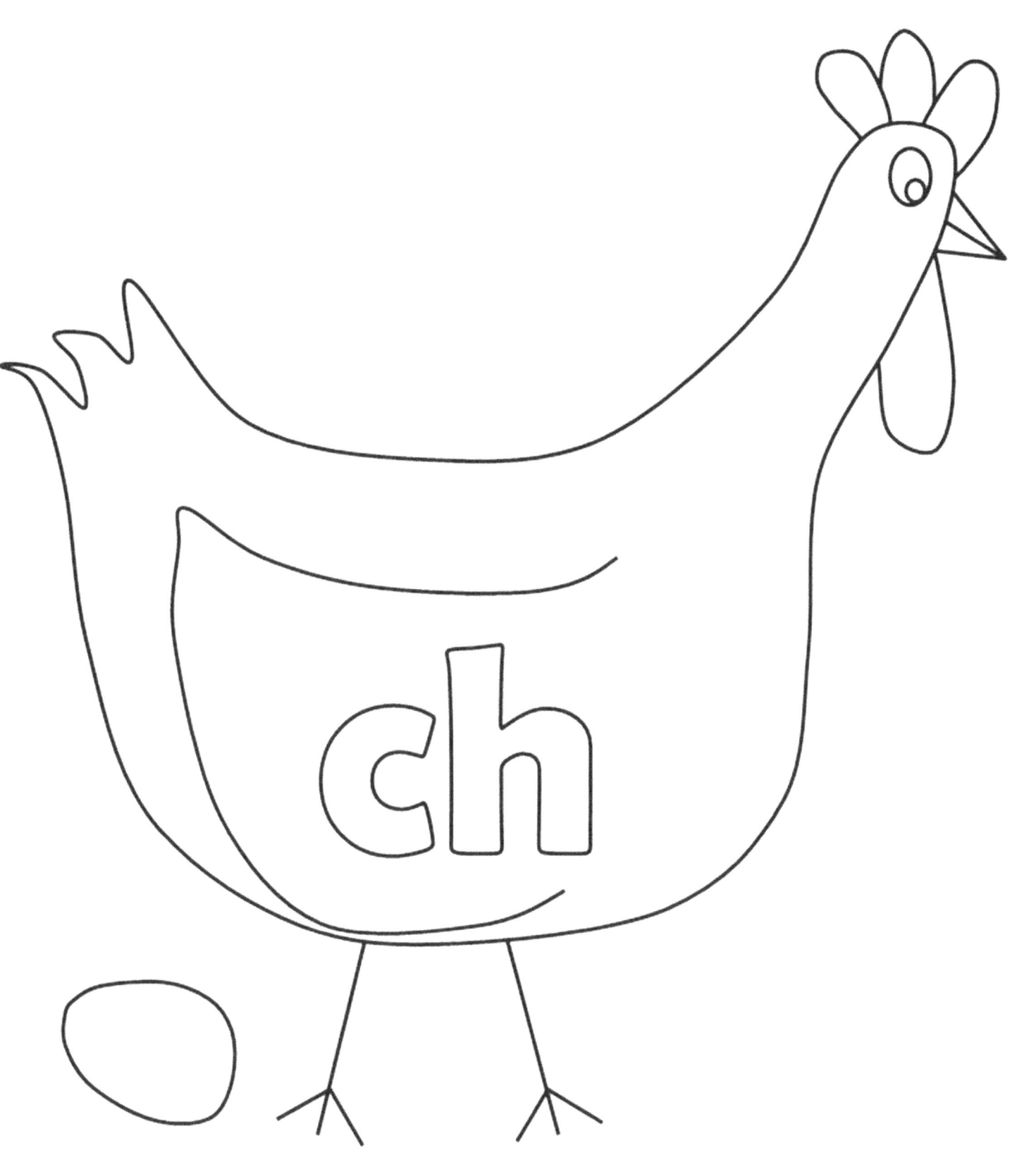

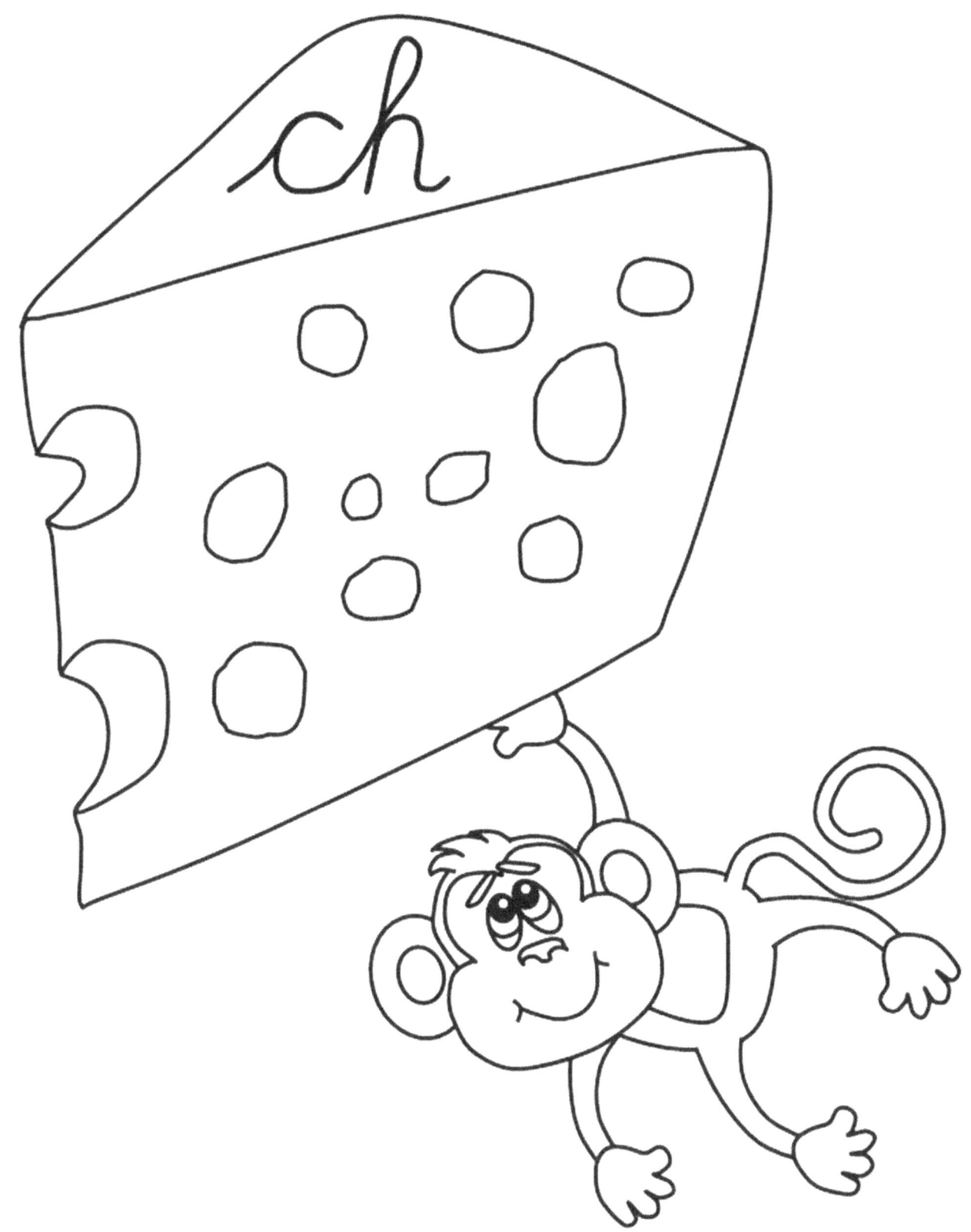

Trace the steps for making the letter c on the following line.

_ch_ _ch_ _ch_ _ch_ _ch_

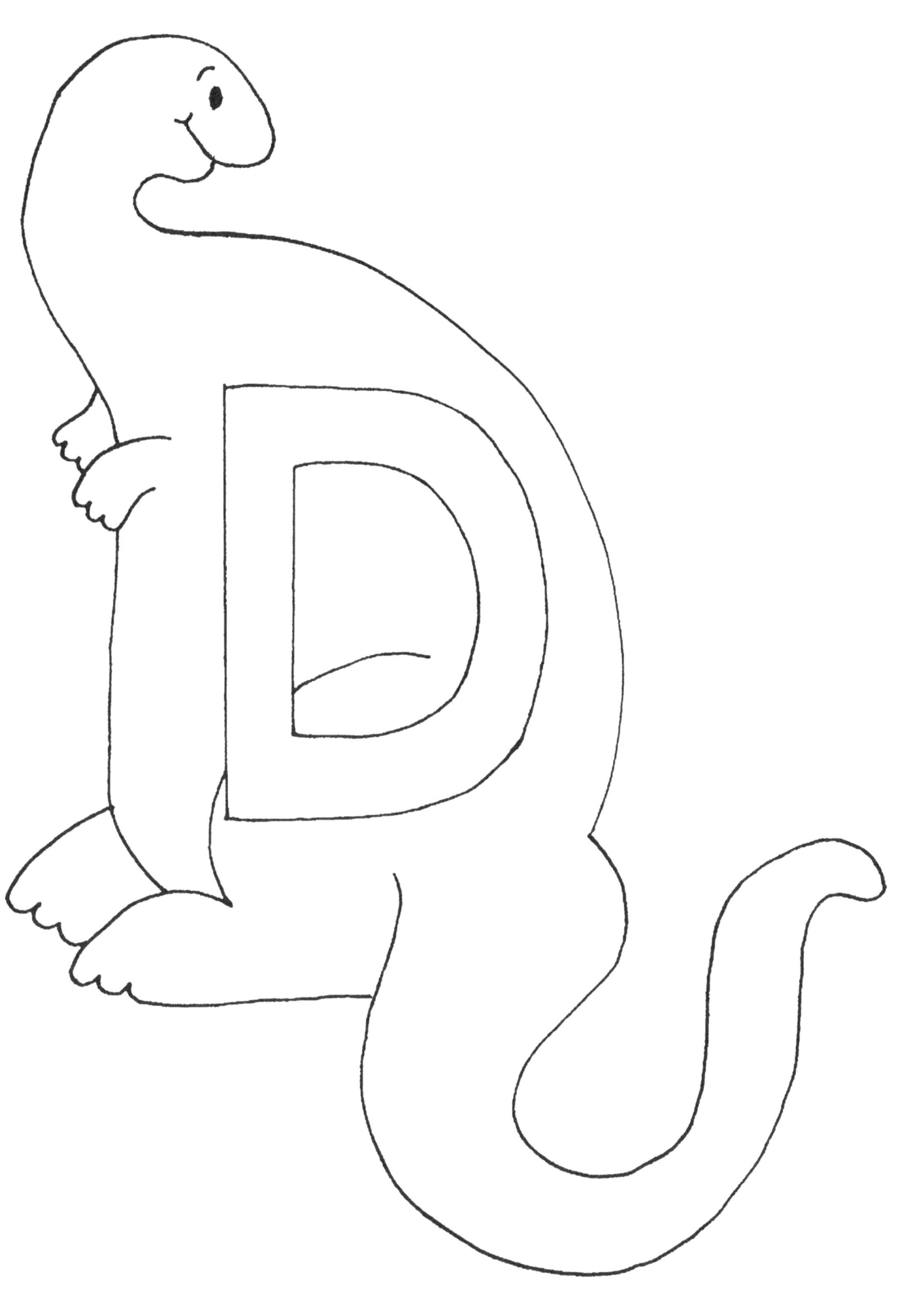

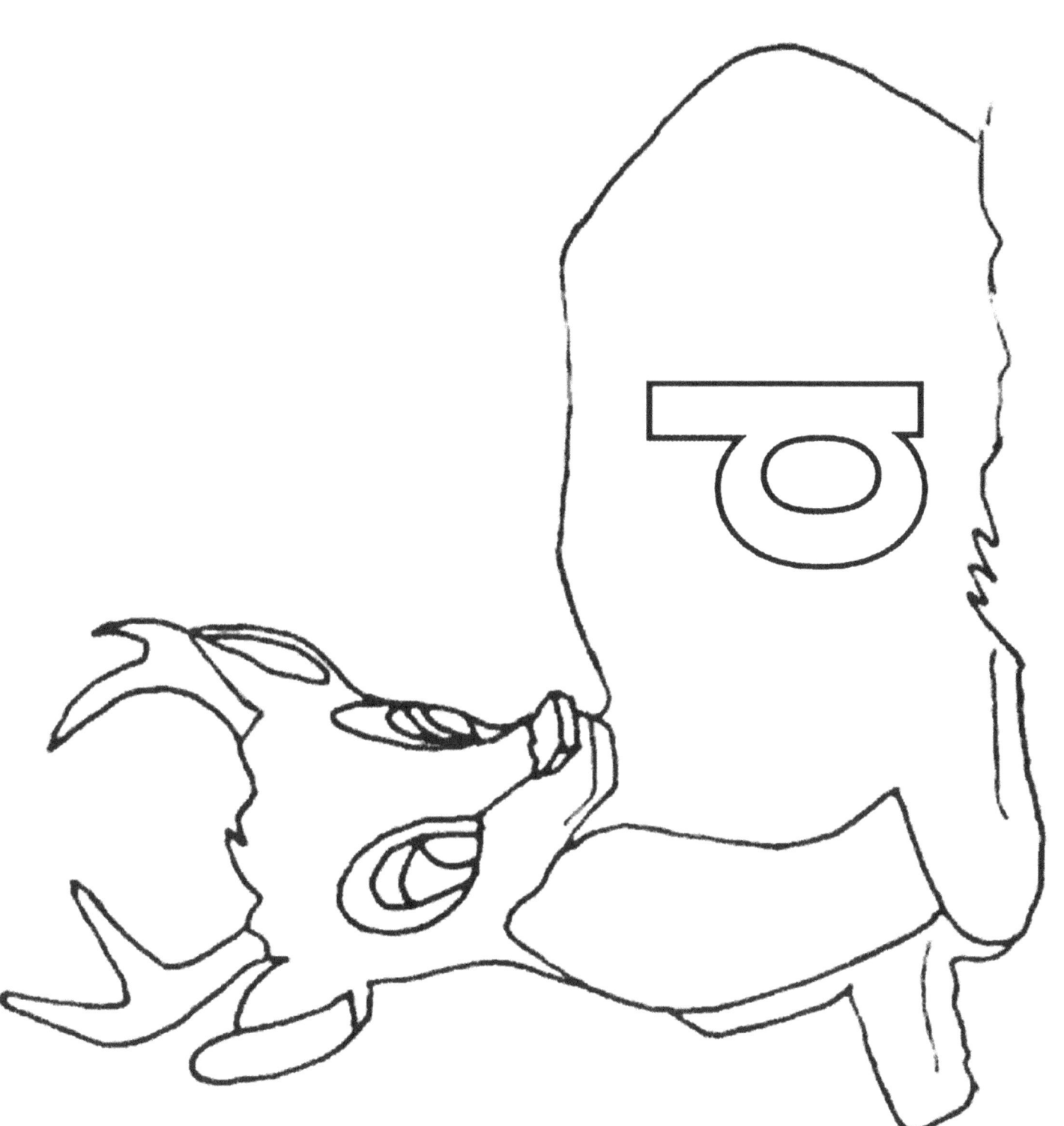

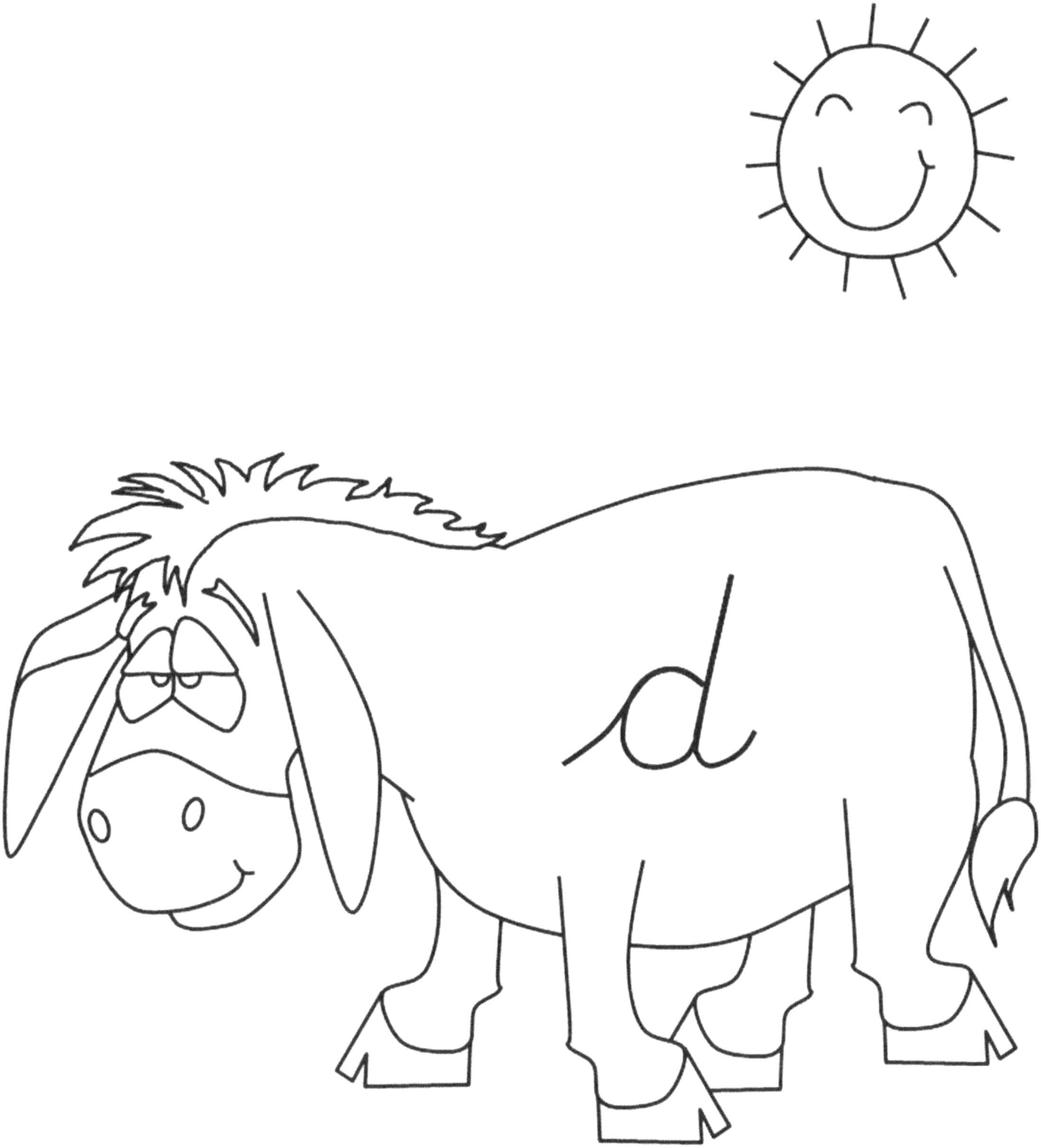

Trace the steps for making the letter d on the following line.

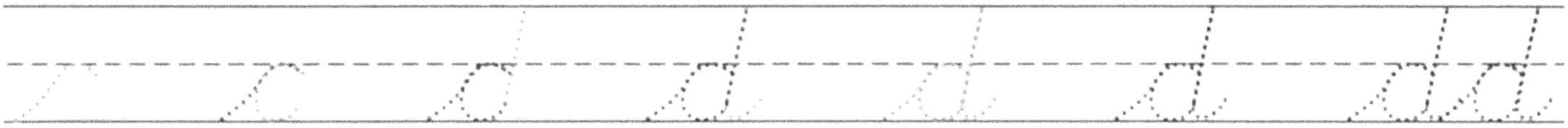

_d_ _d_ _d_ _d_ _d_ _dd_

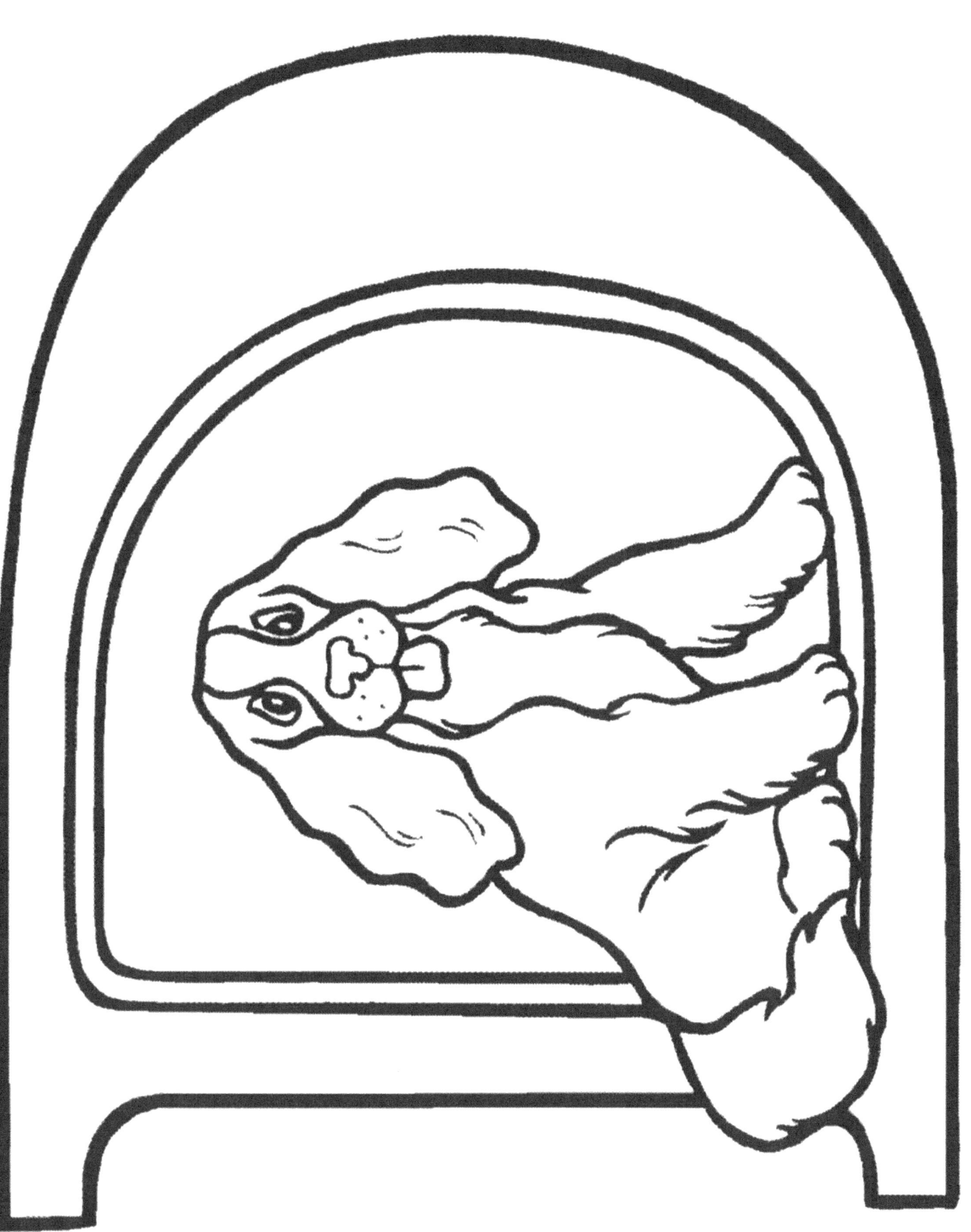

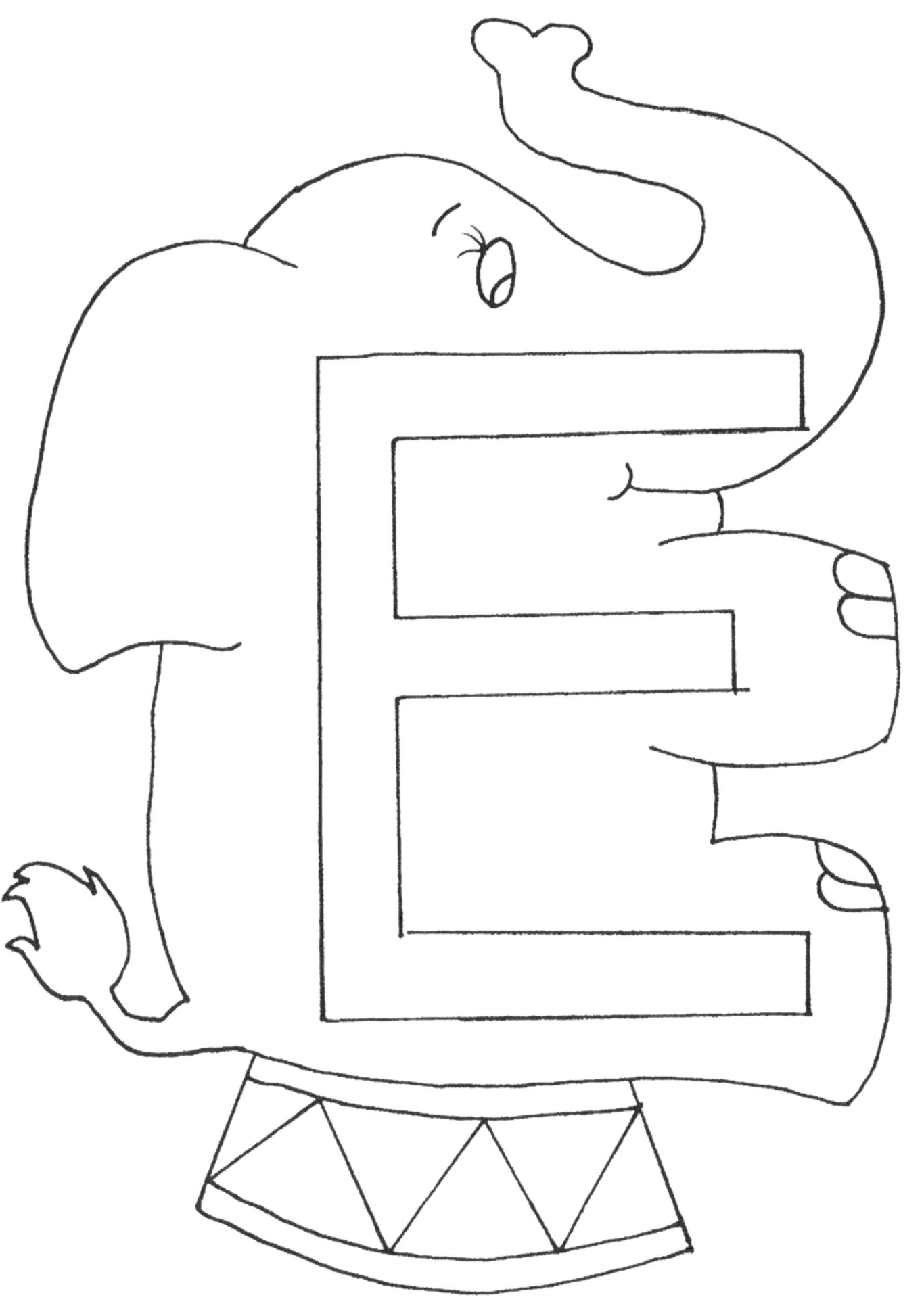

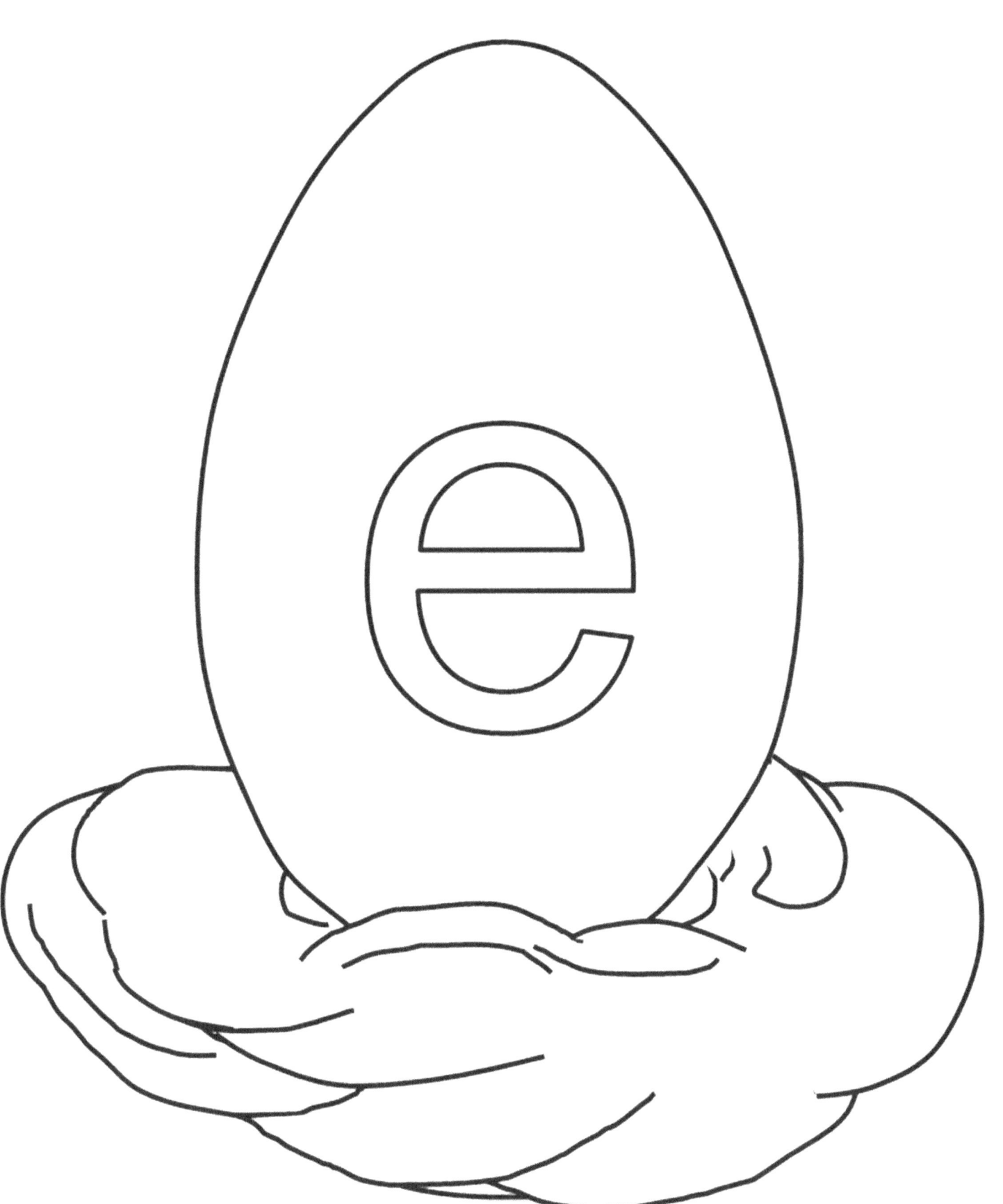

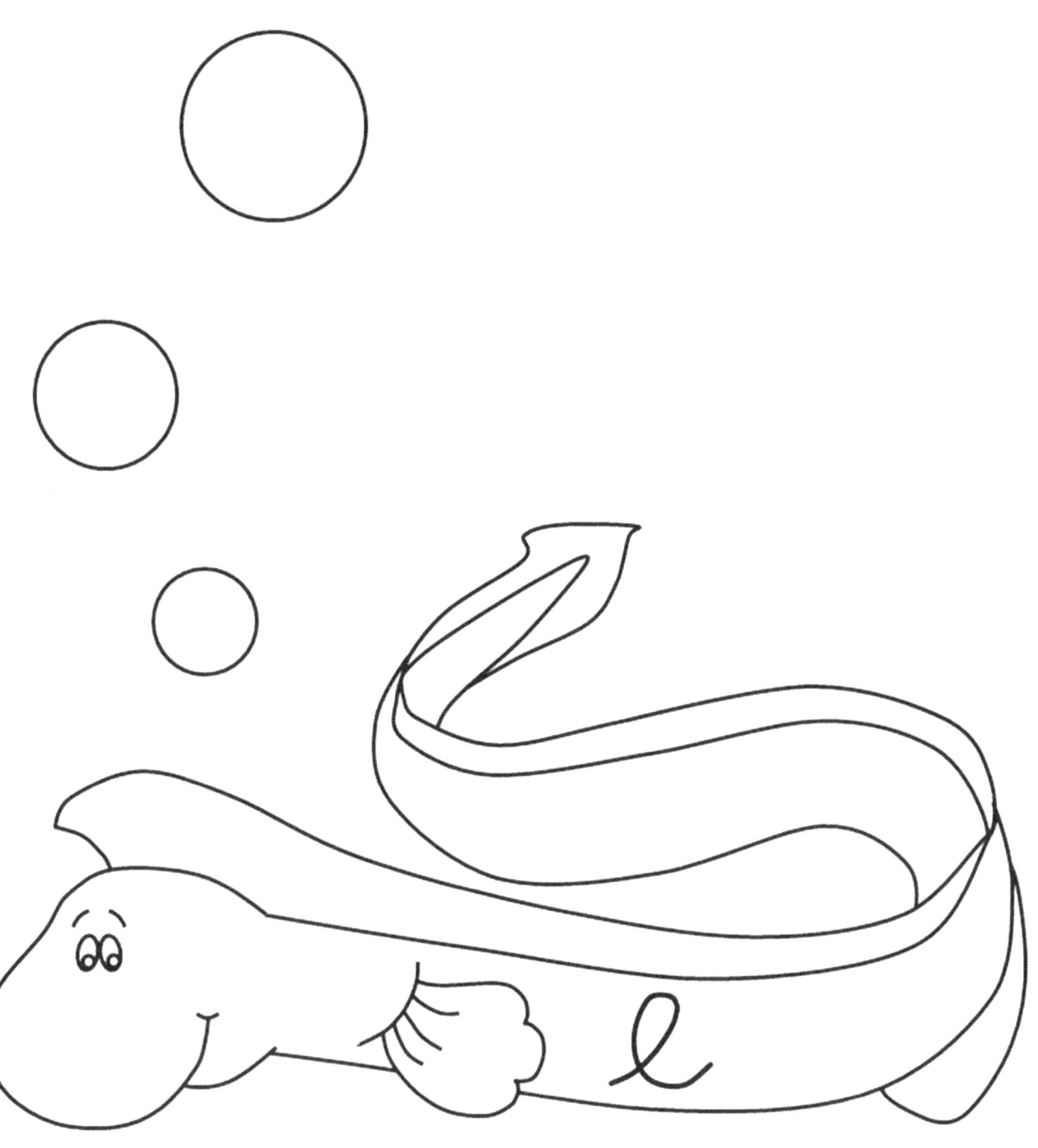

Trace the steps for making the letter e on the following line.

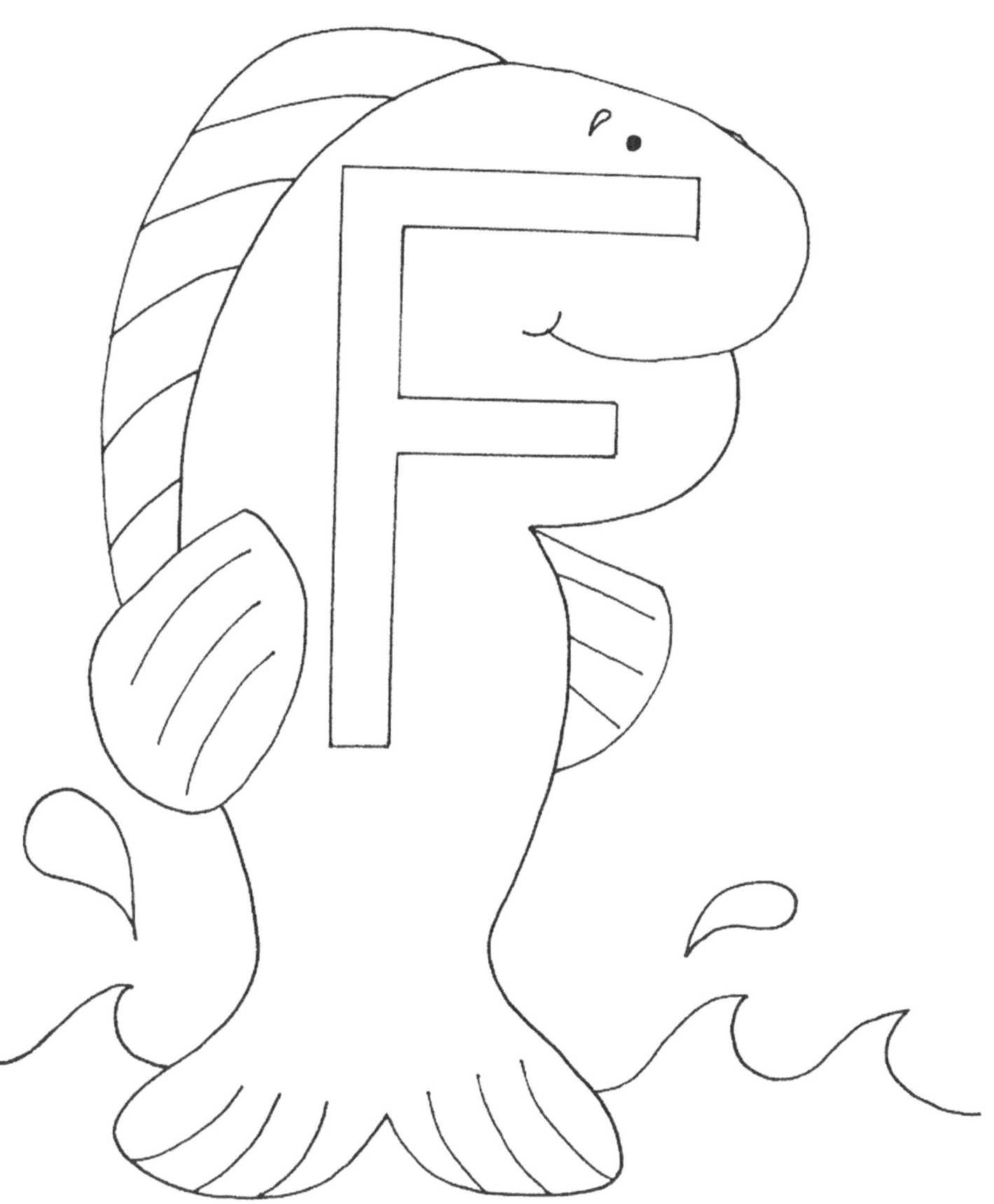

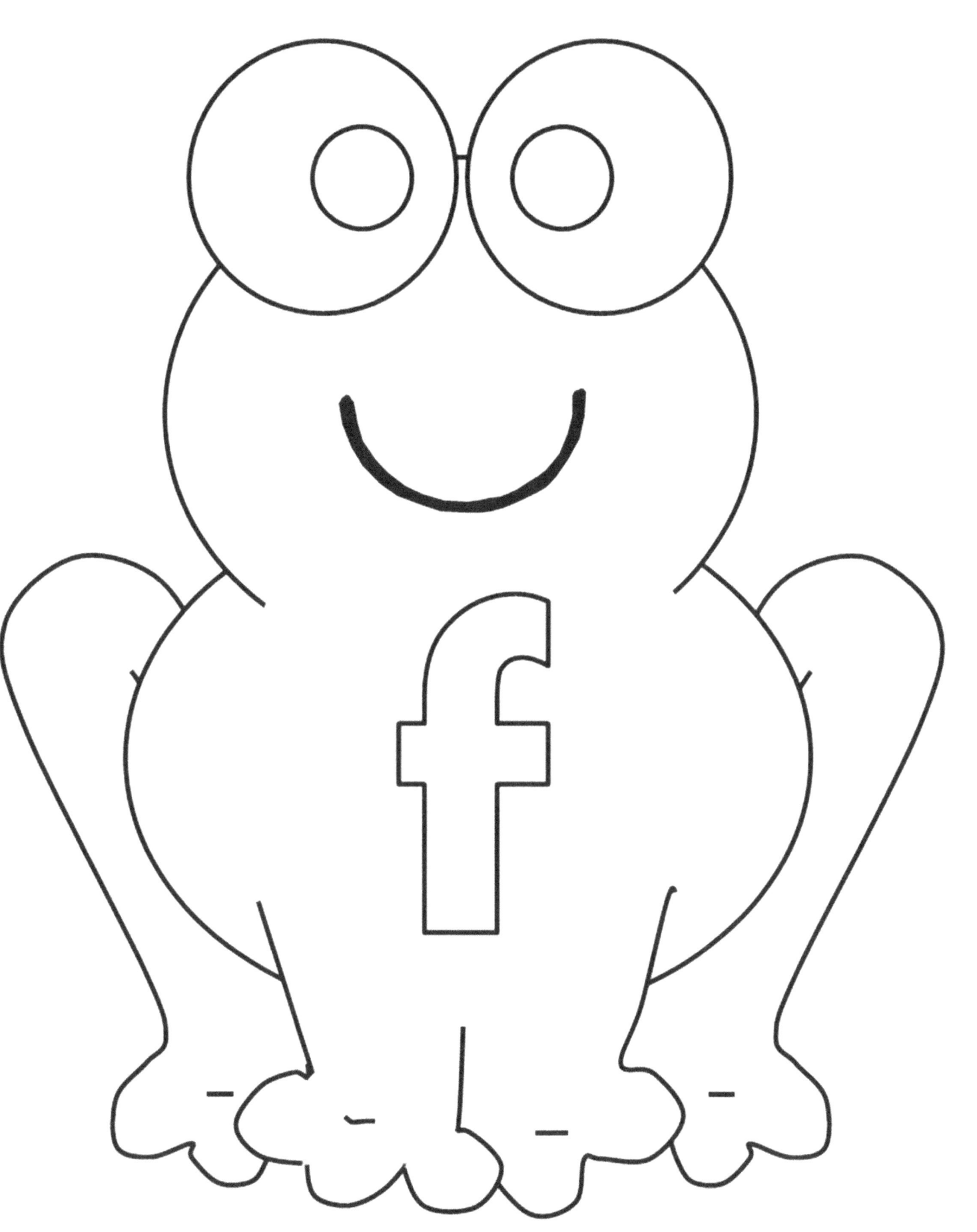

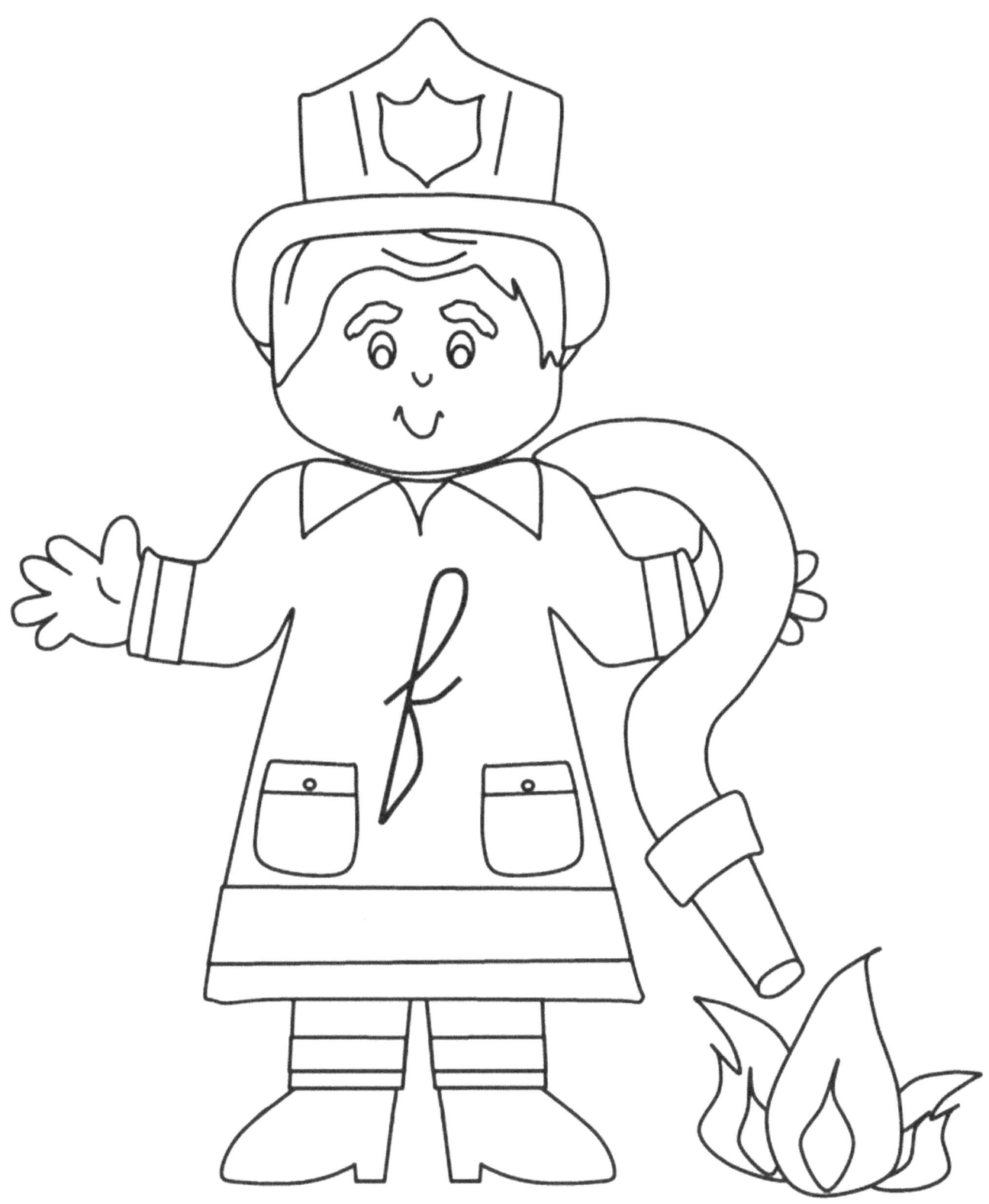

Trace the steps for making the letter f on the following line.

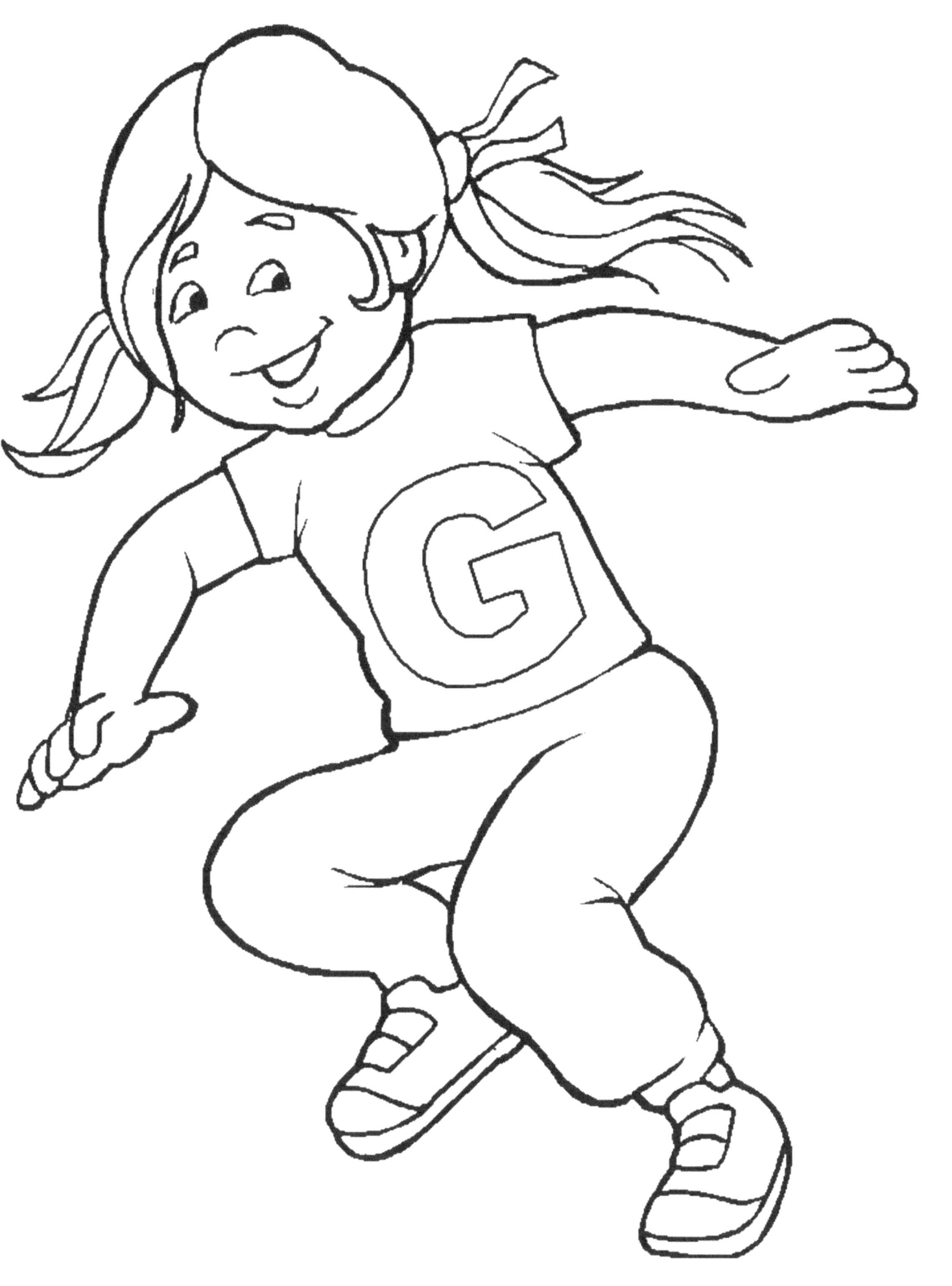

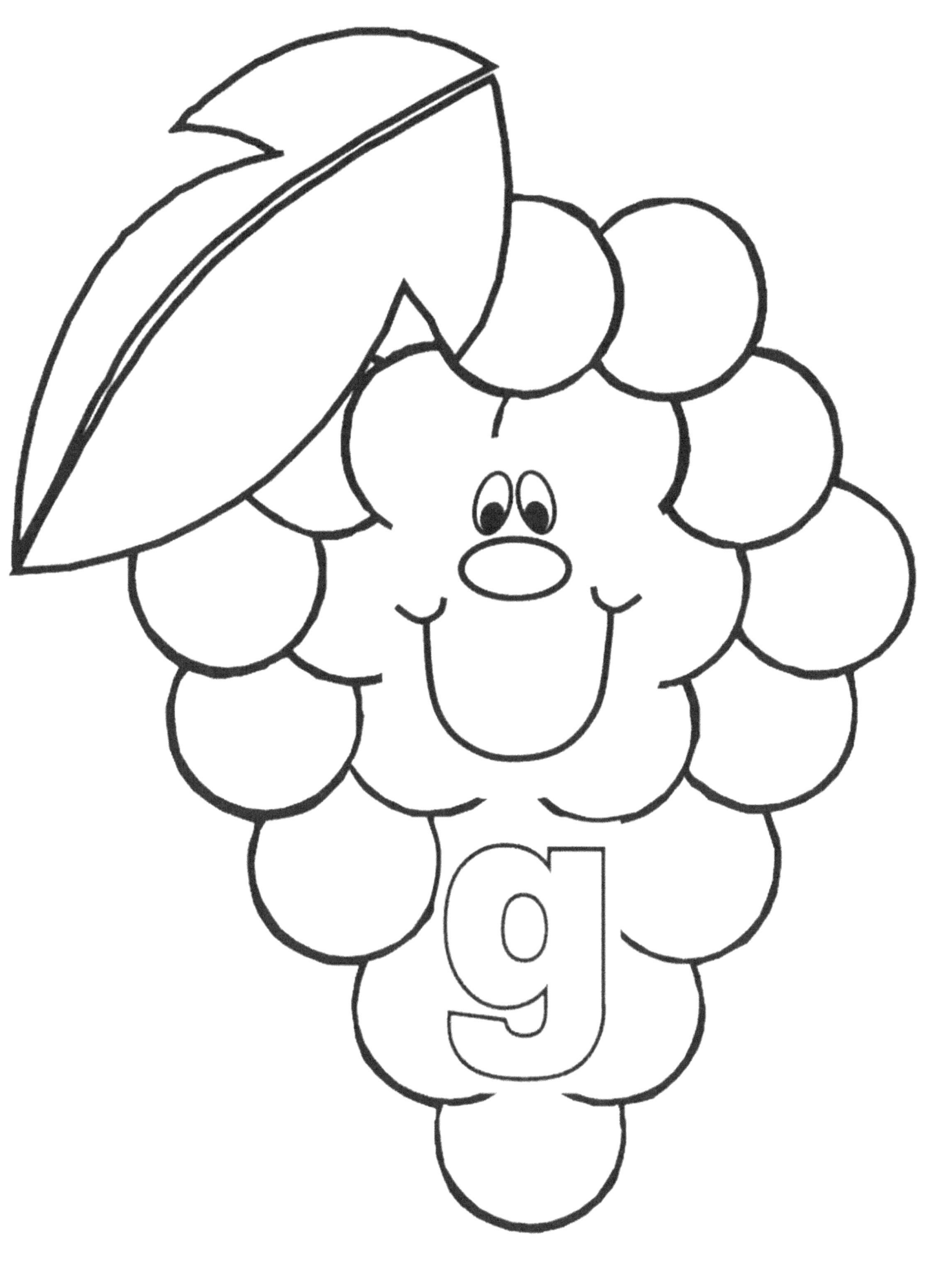

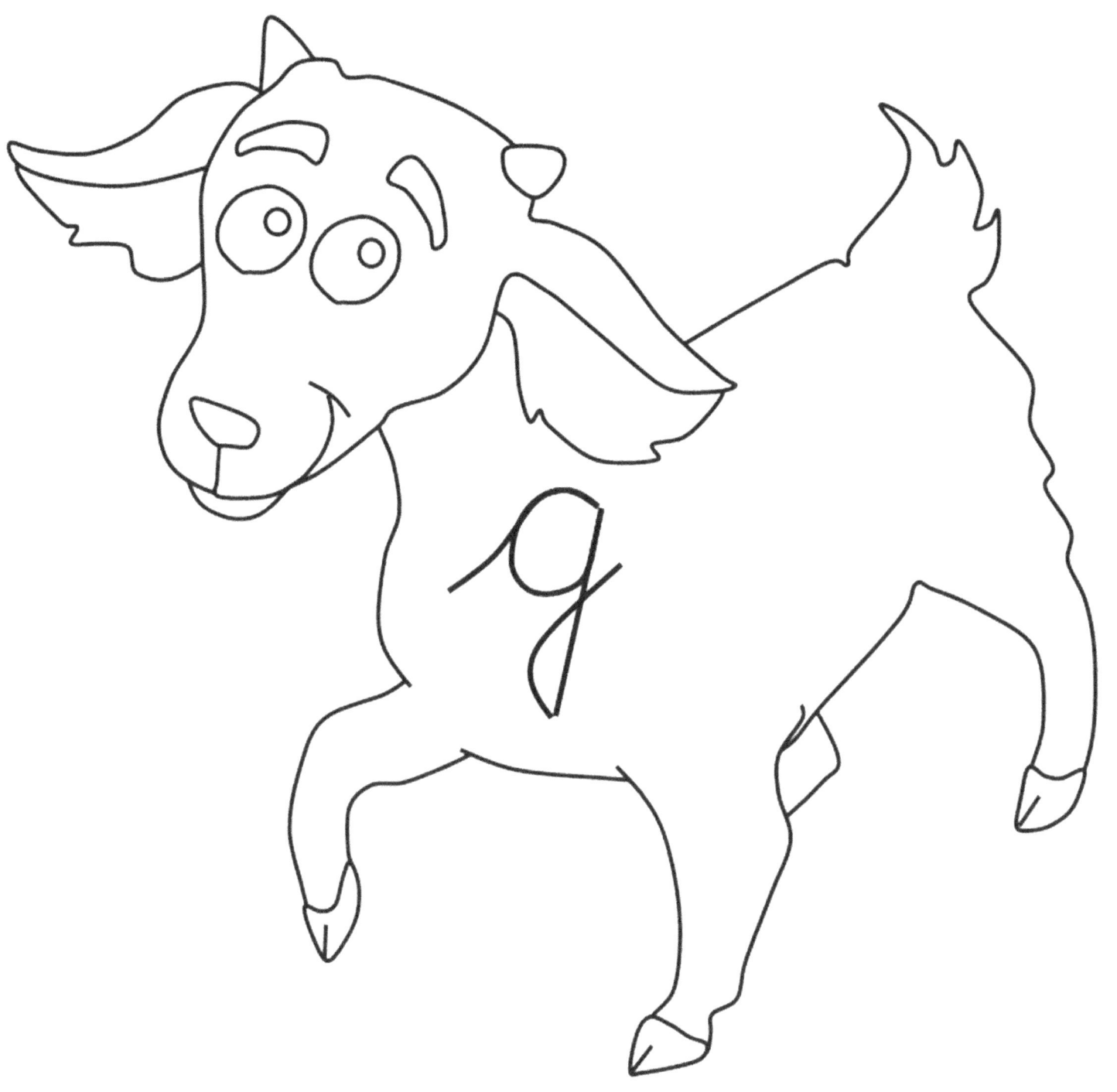

Trace the steps for making the letter g on the following line.

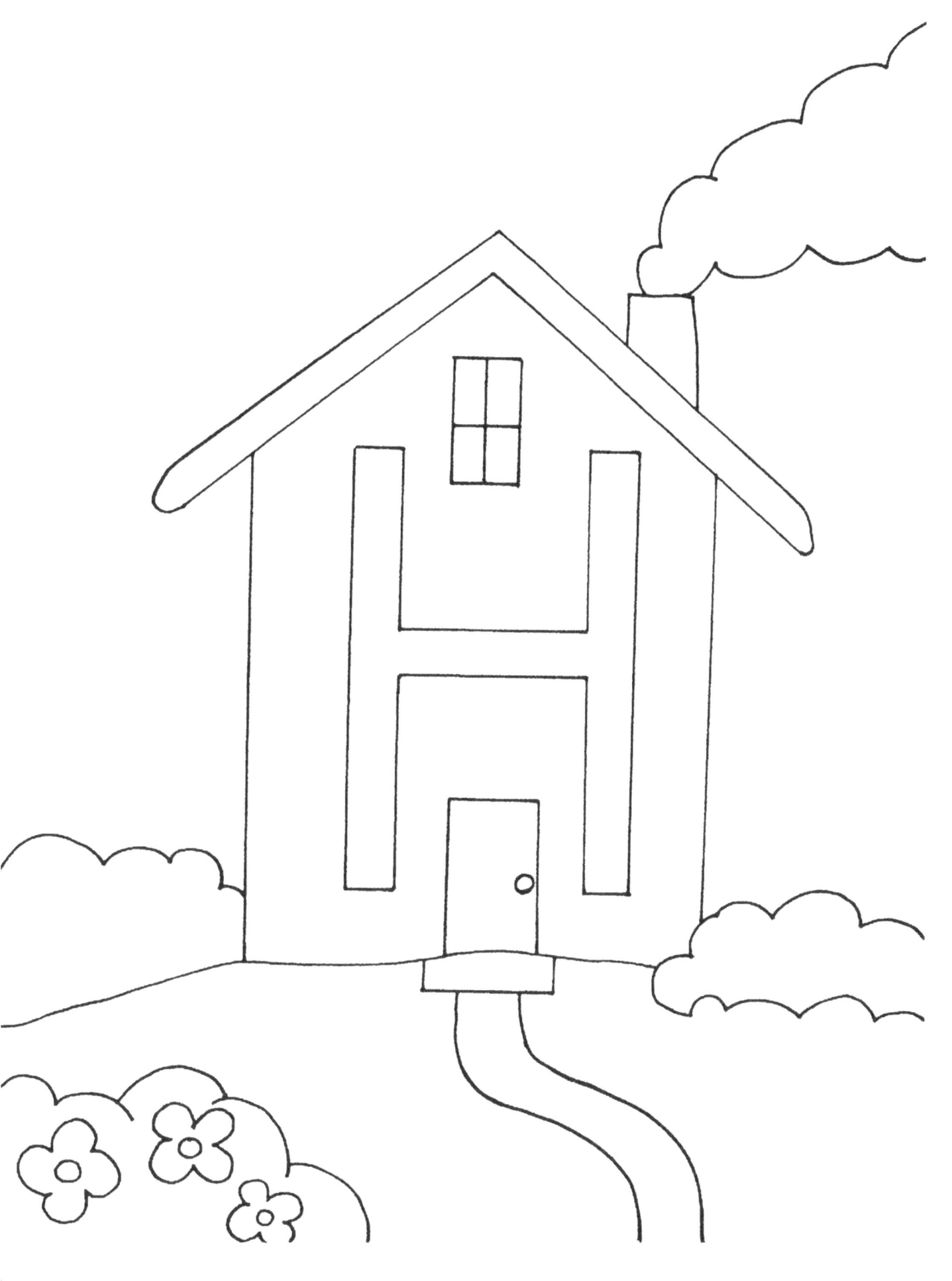

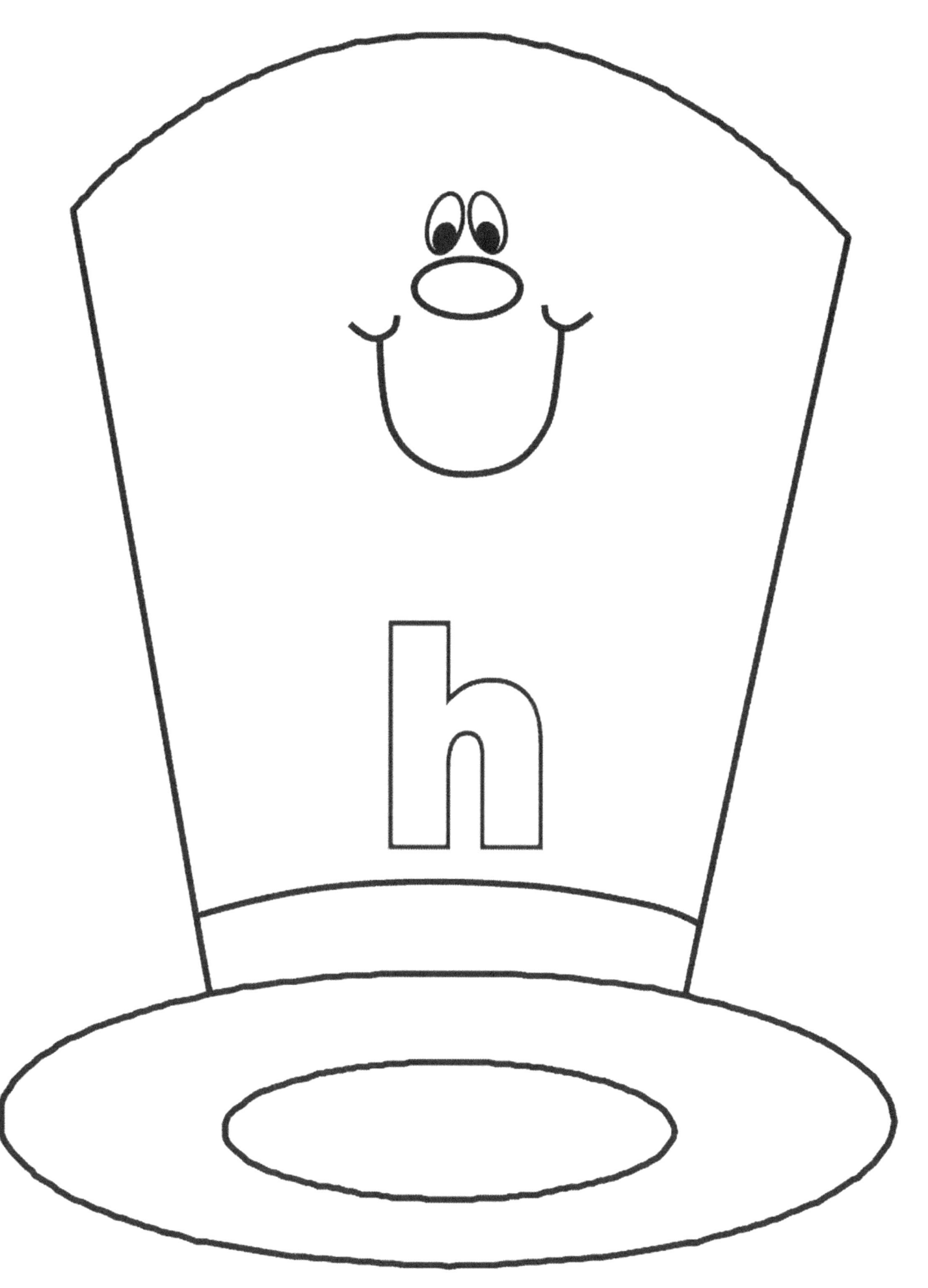

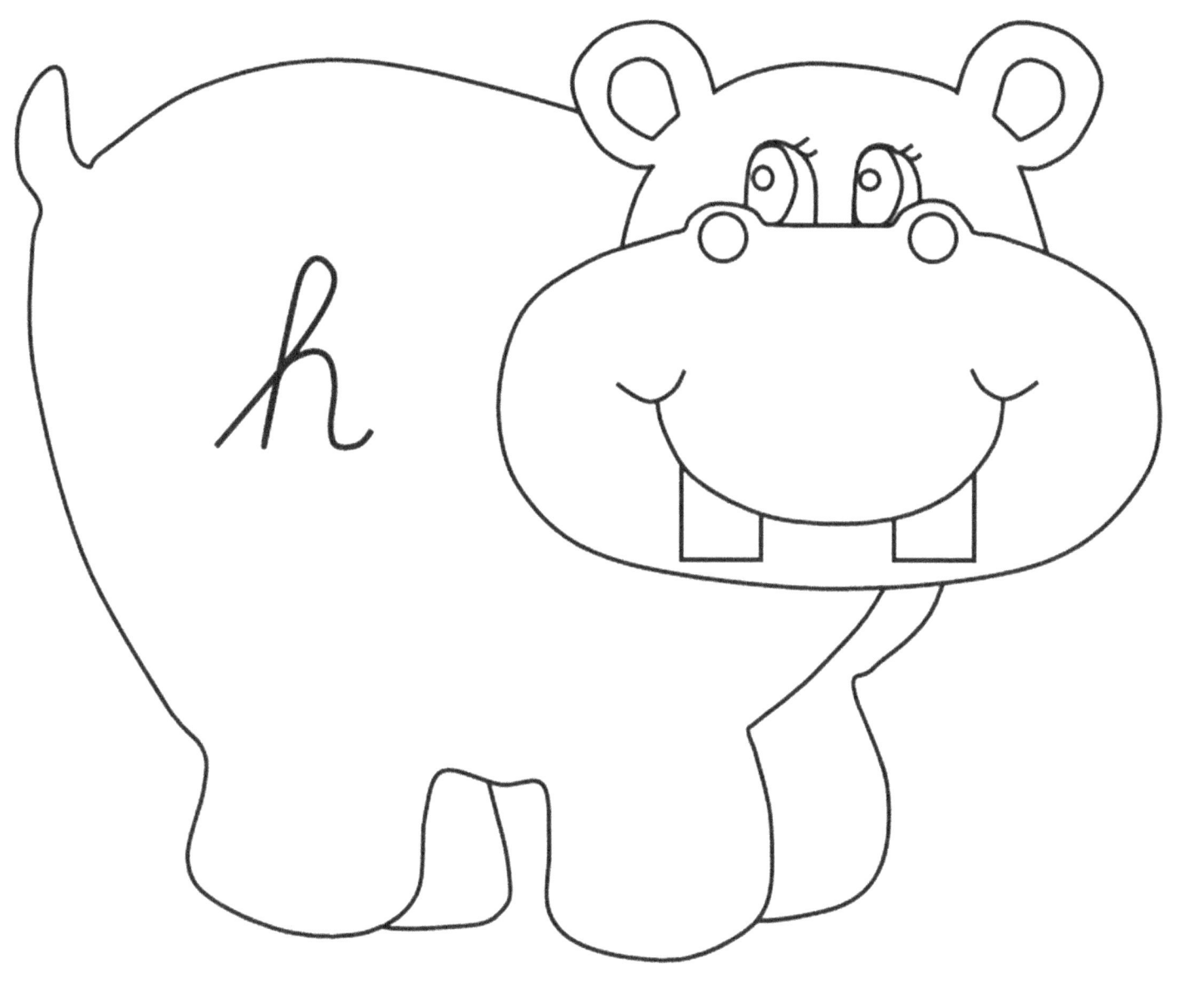

Trace the steps for making the letter h on the following line.

_h_ _h_ _h_ _h_ _h_ _h_ _hh_

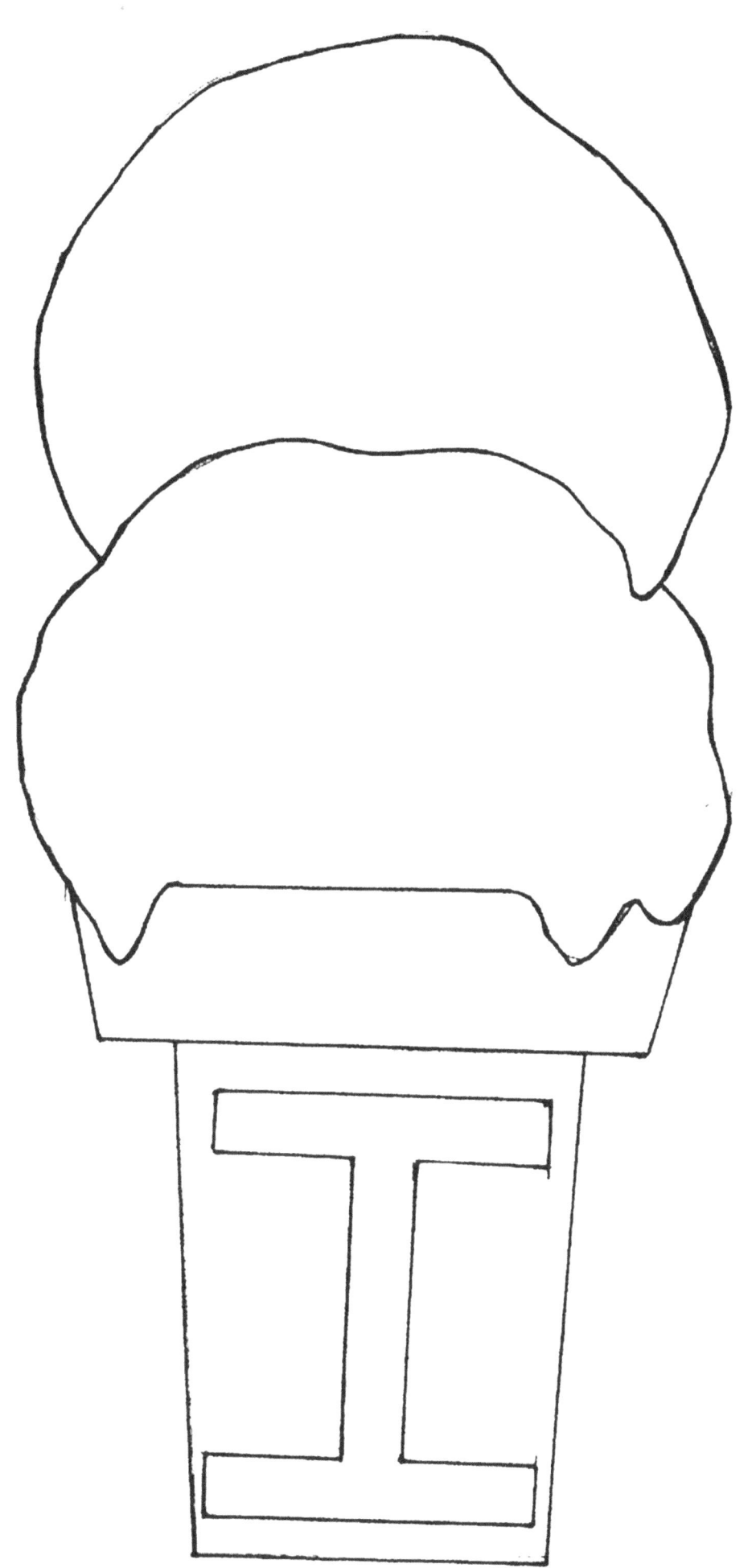

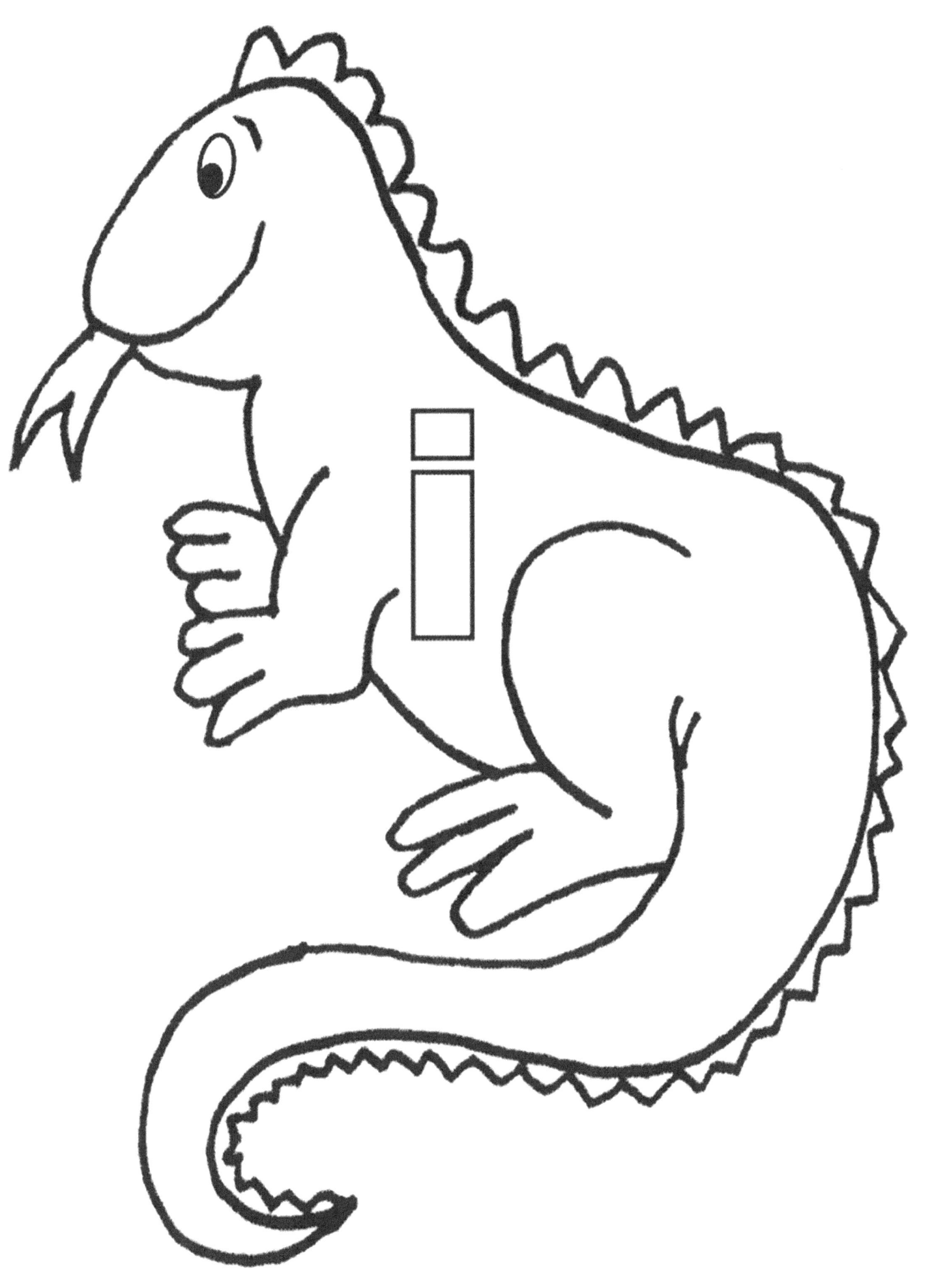

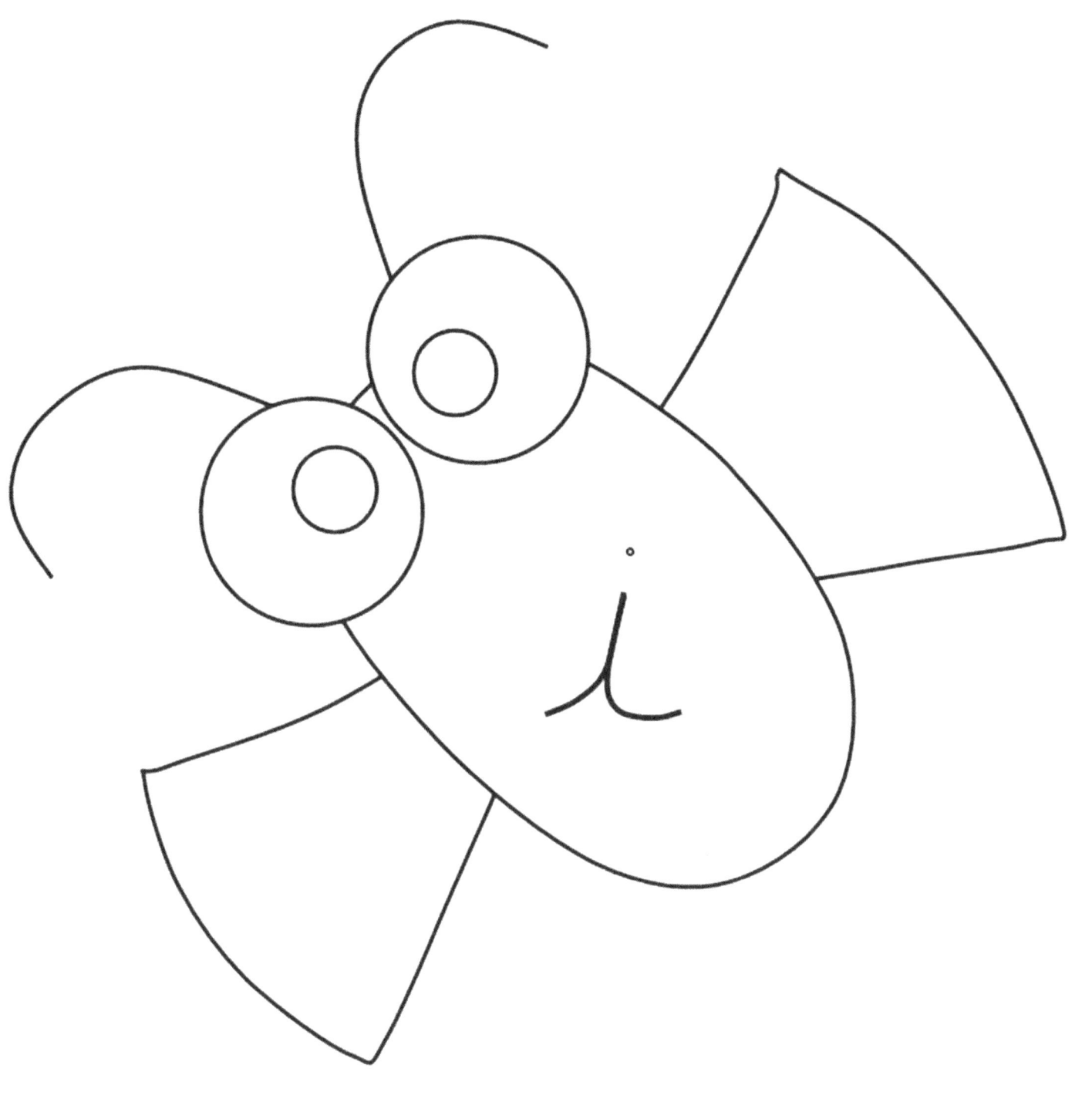

Trace the steps for making the letter i on the following line.

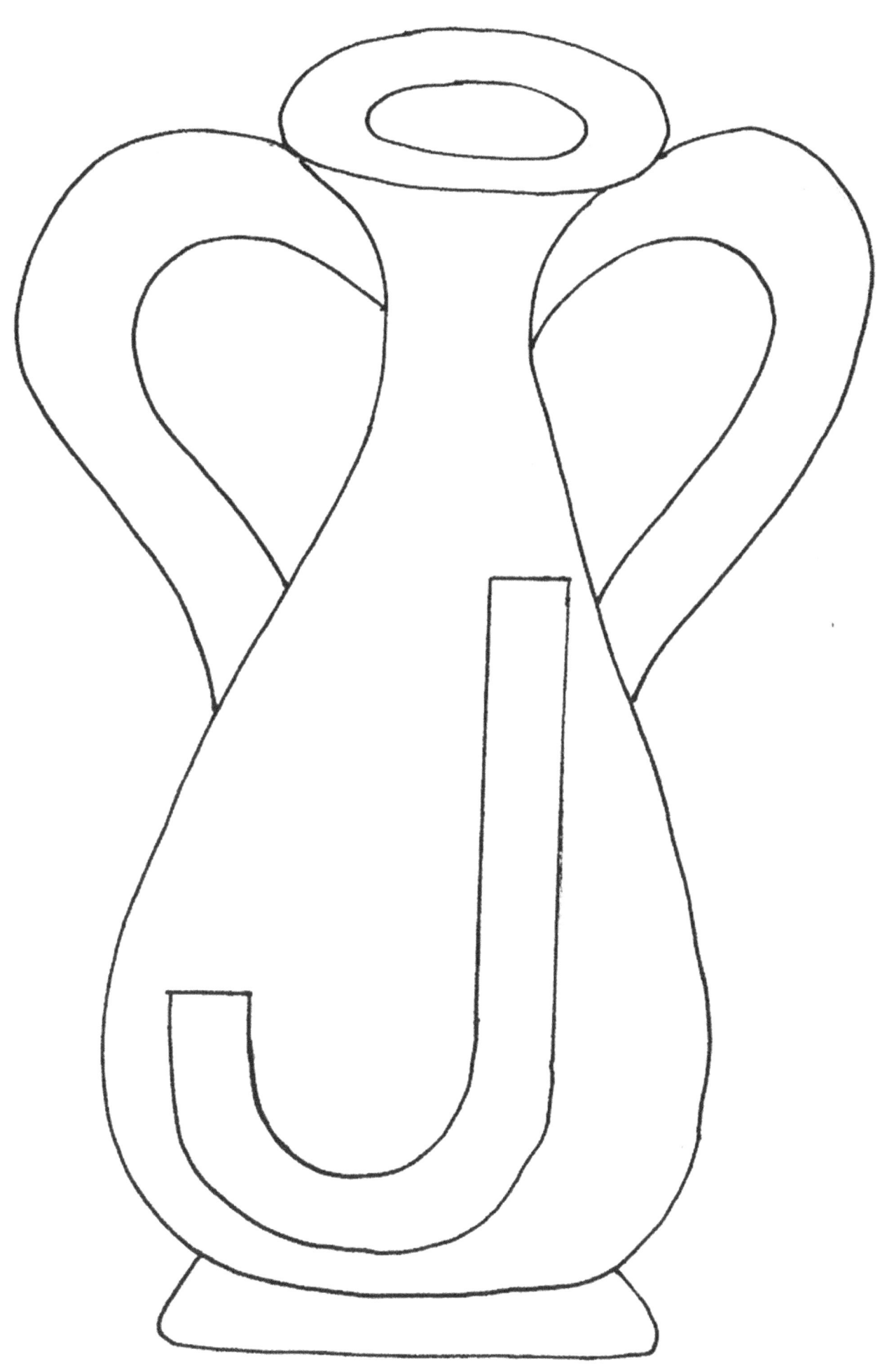

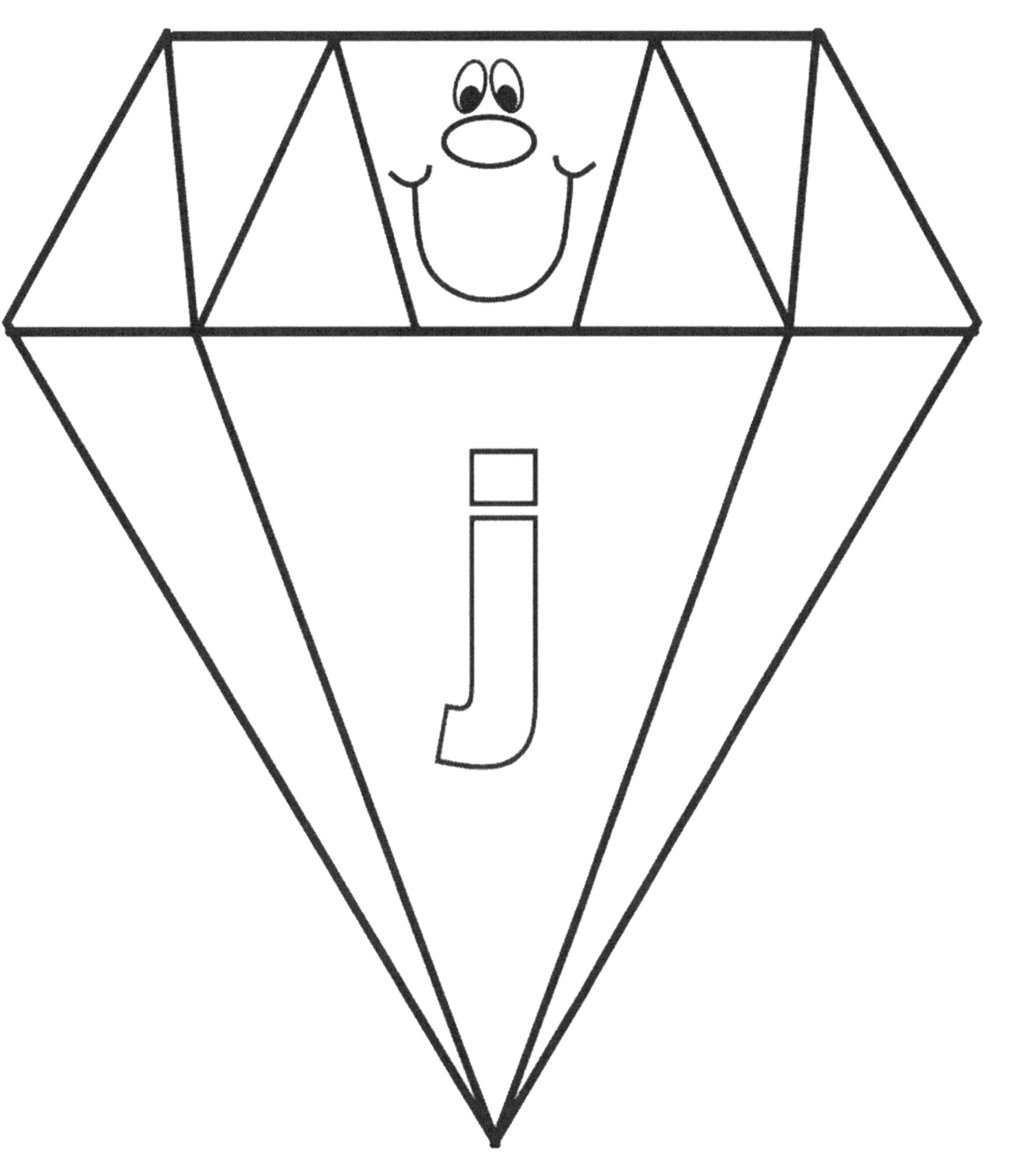

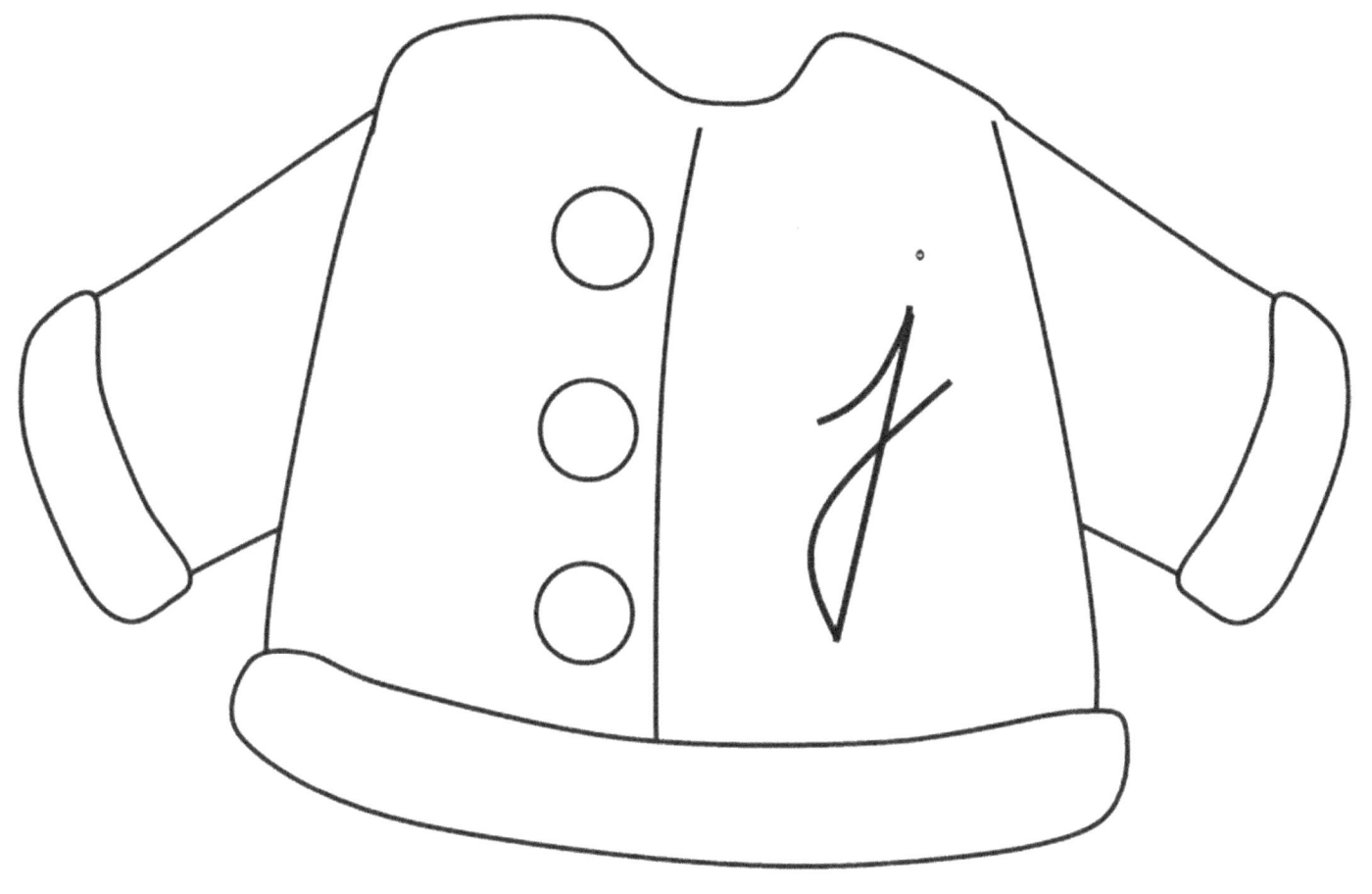

Trace the steps for making the letter j on the following line.

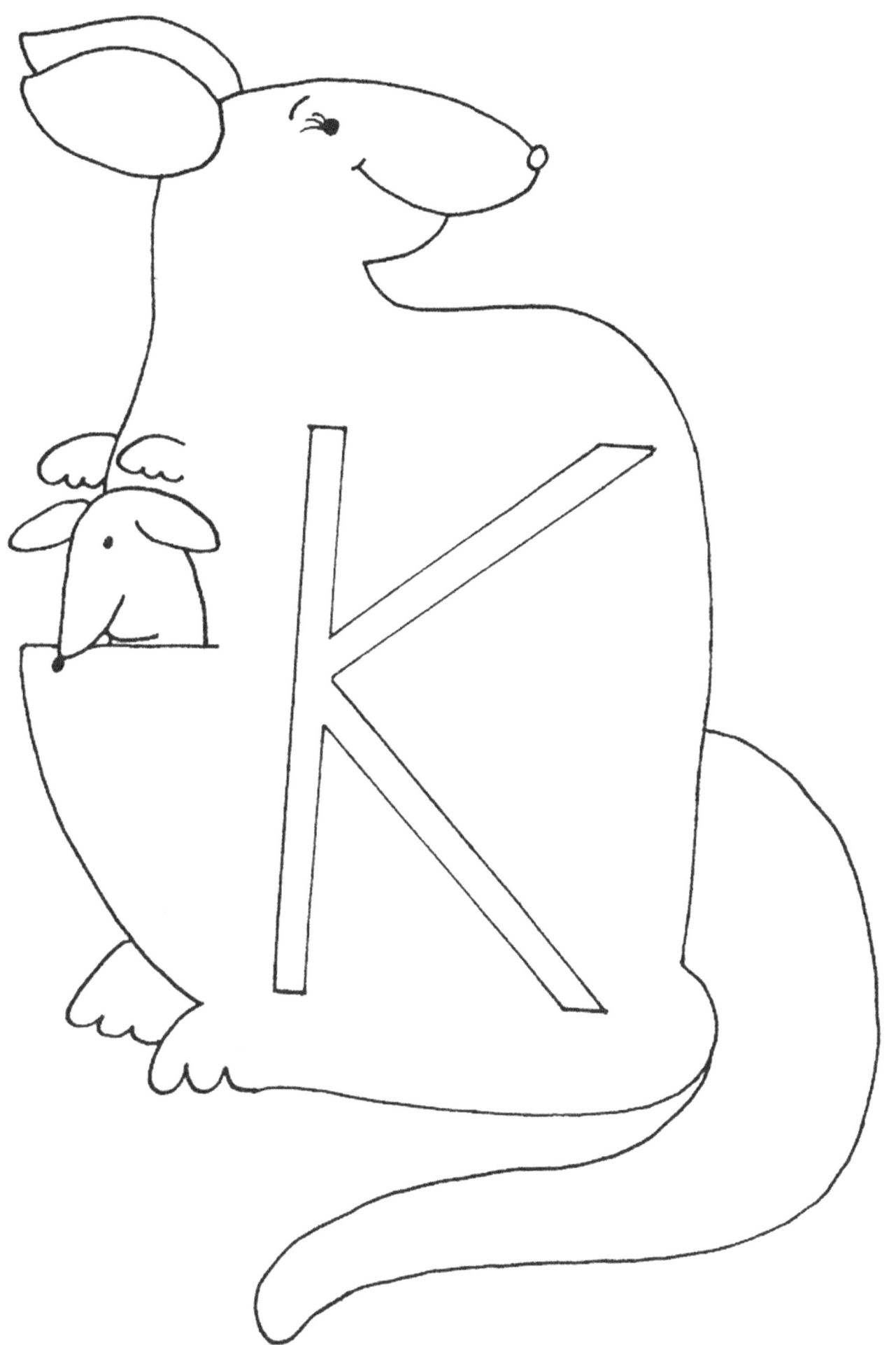

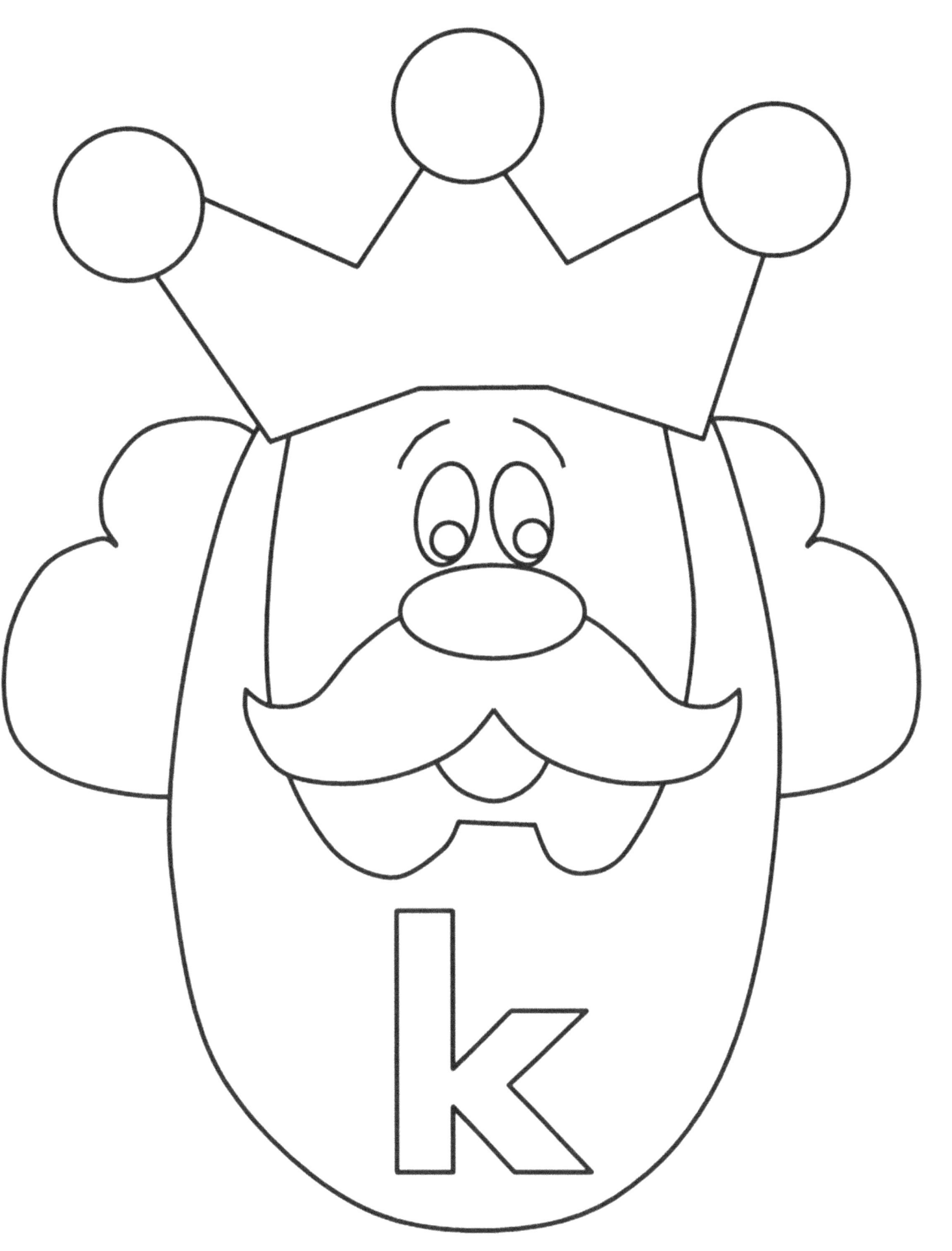

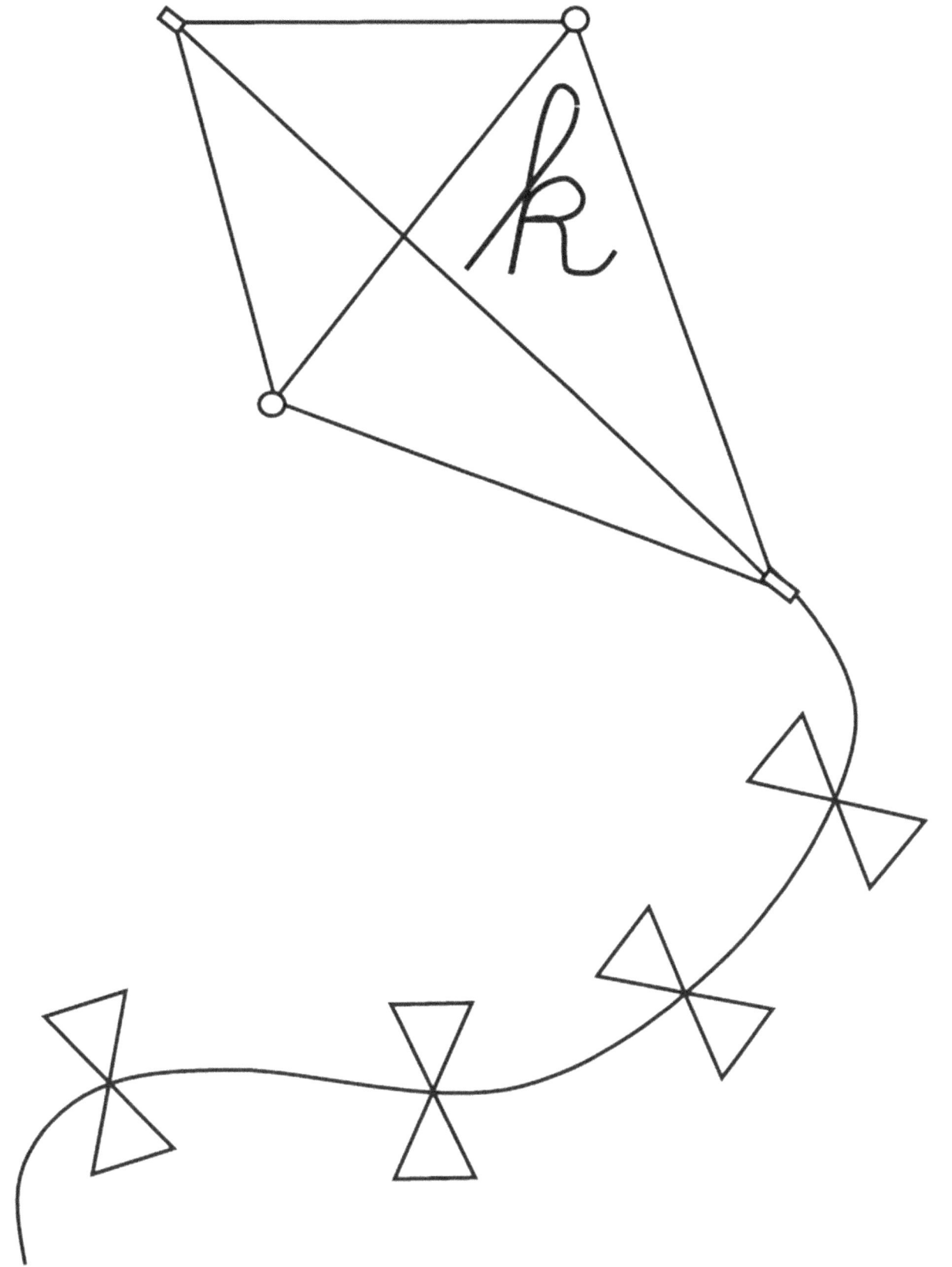

Trace the steps for making the letter k on the following line.

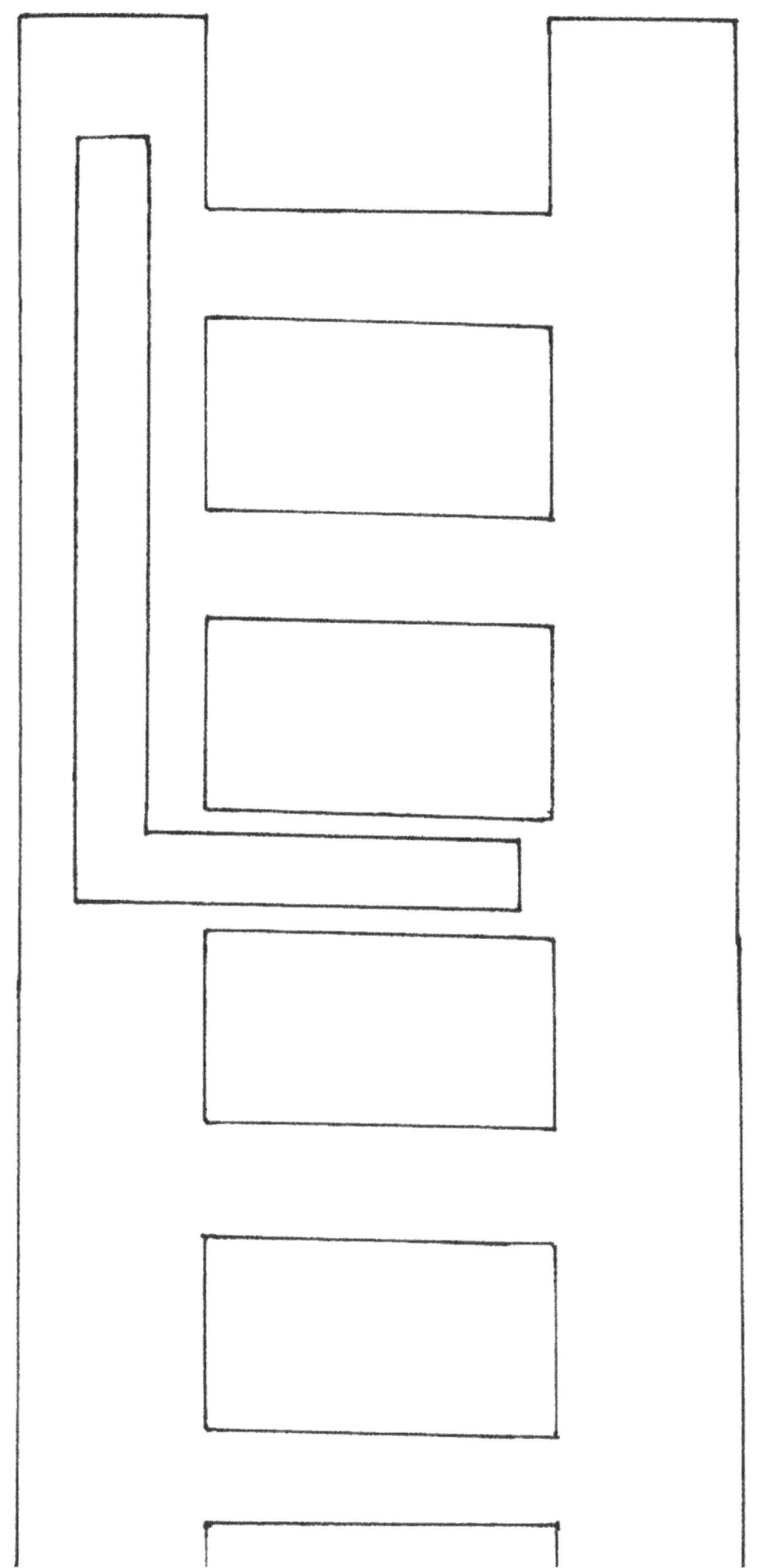

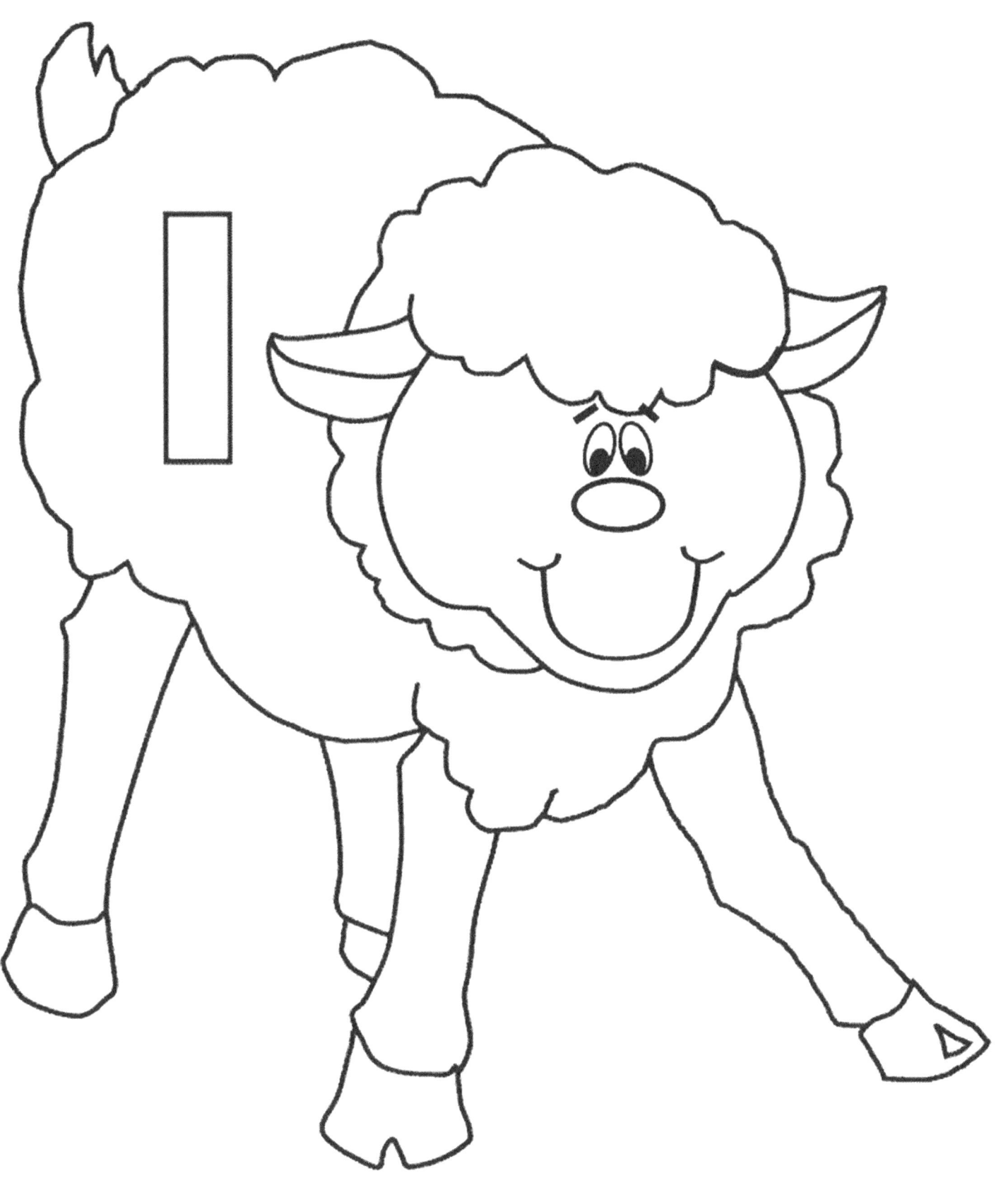

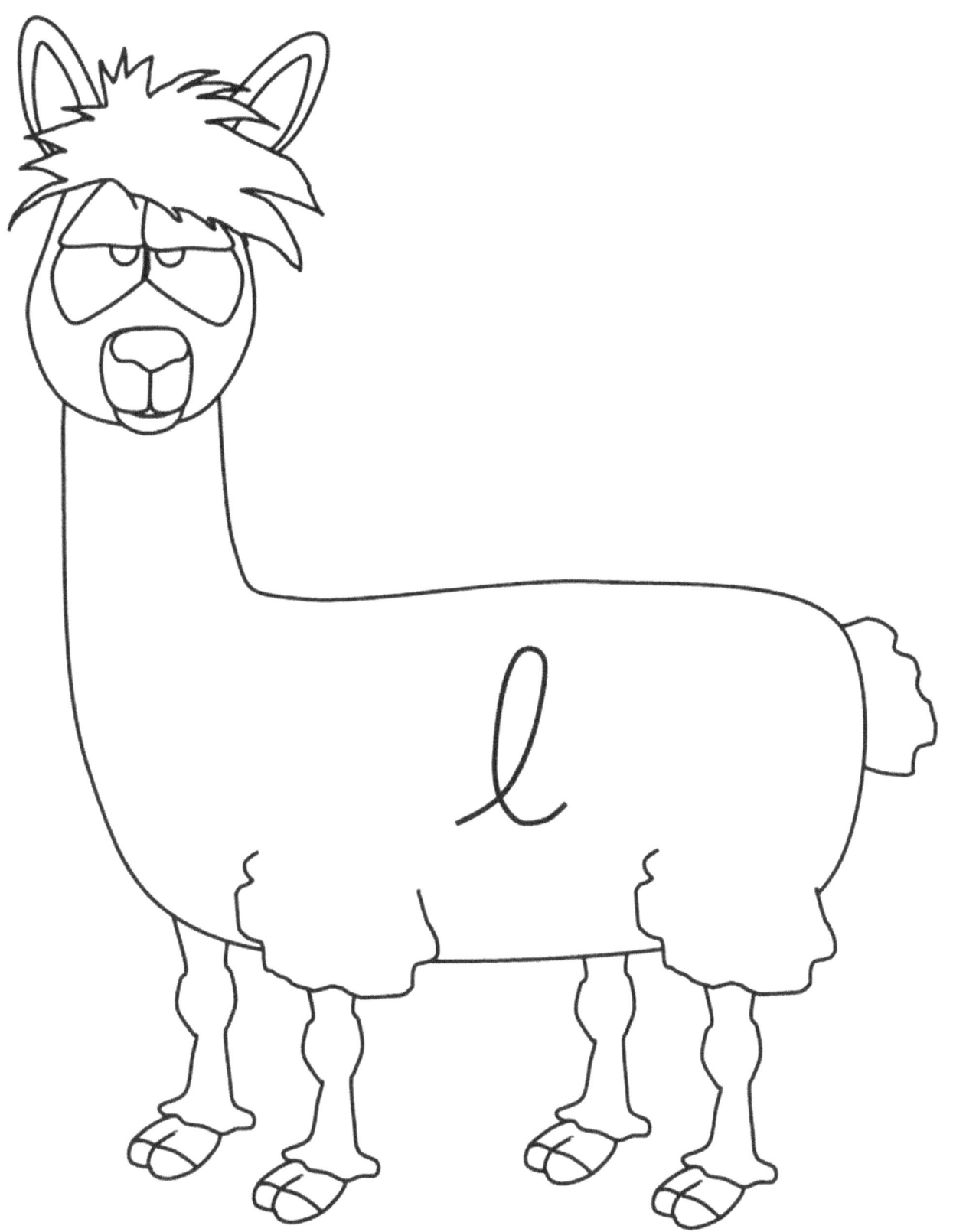

Trace the steps for making the letter l on the following line.

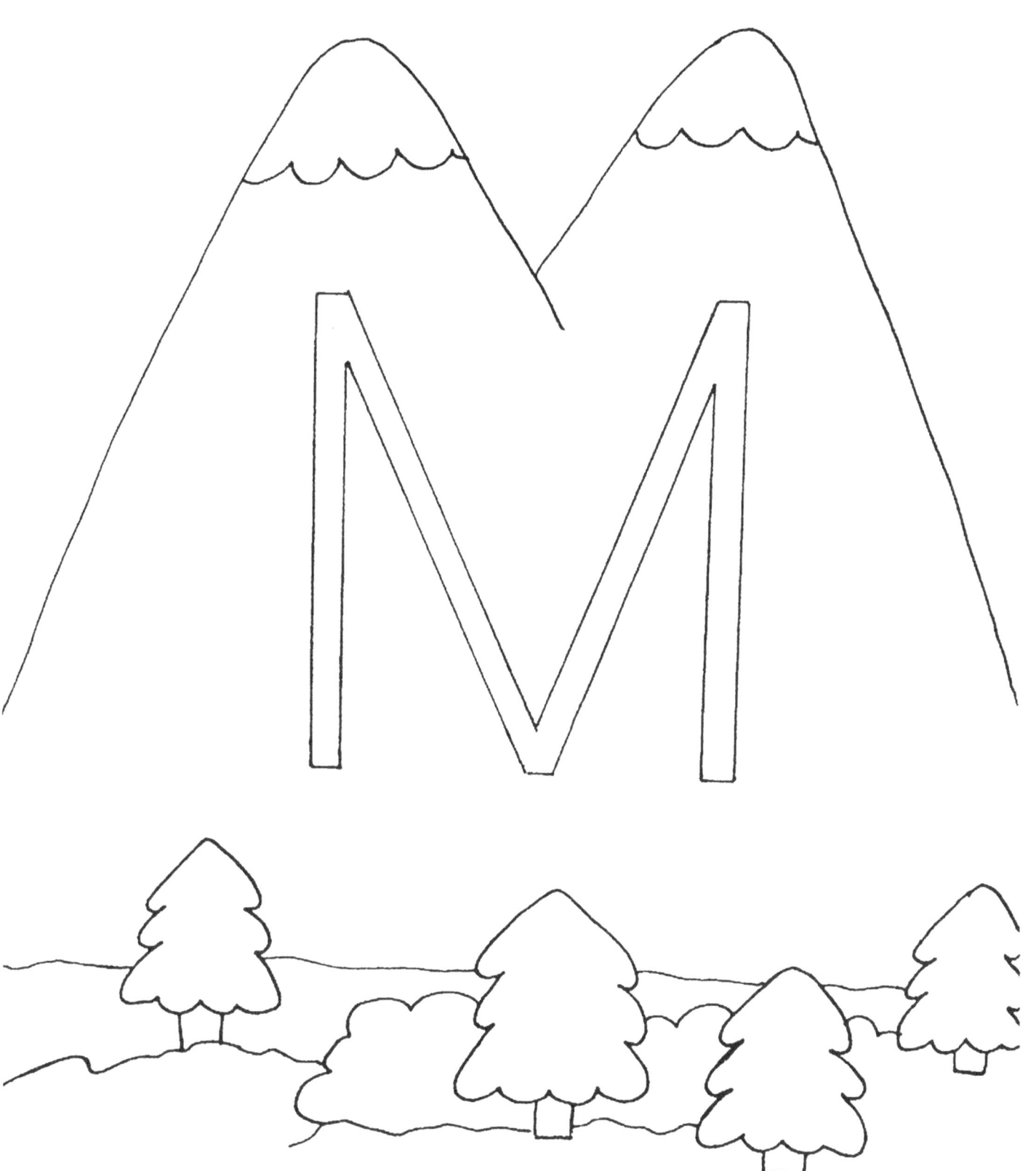

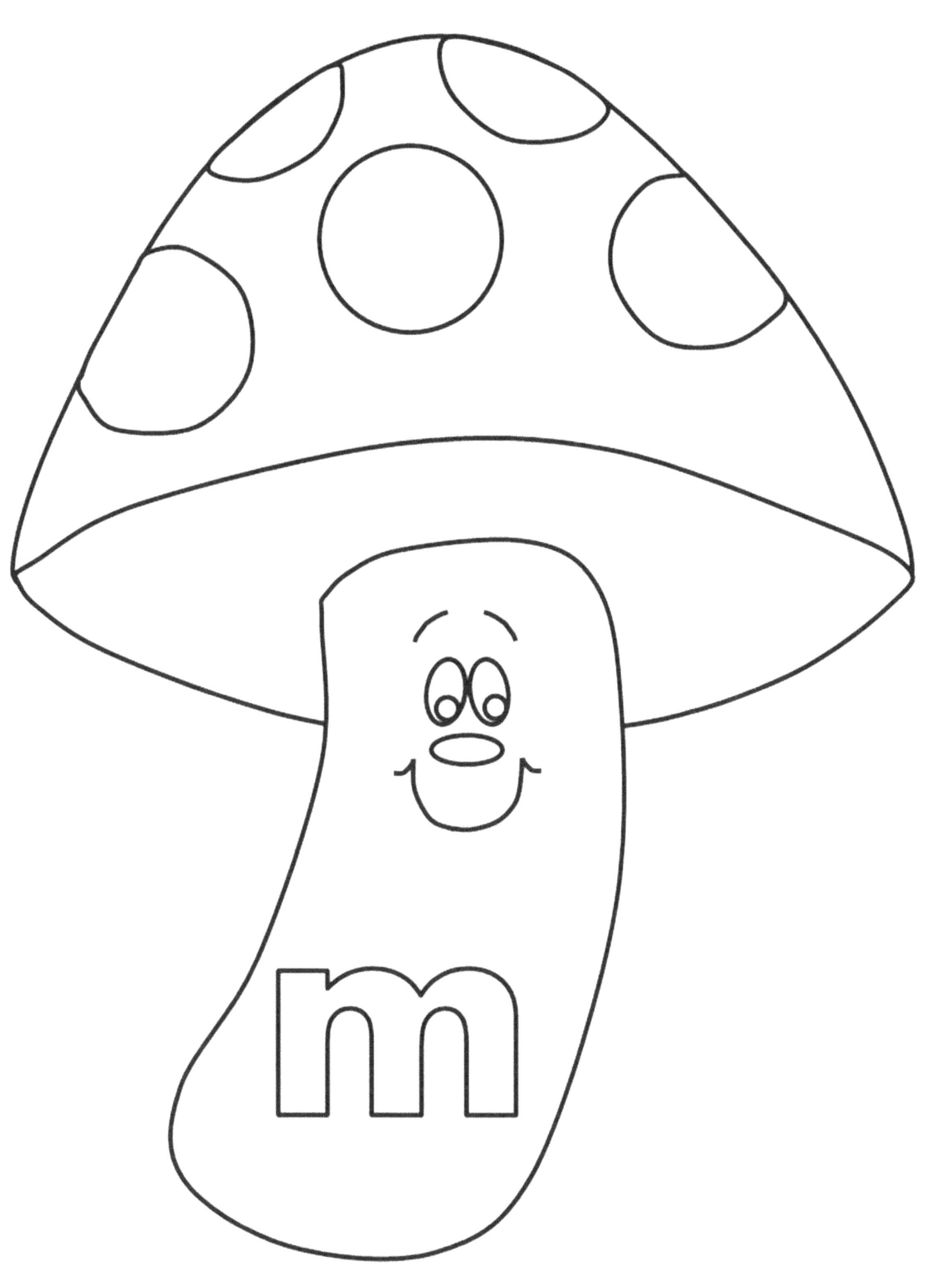

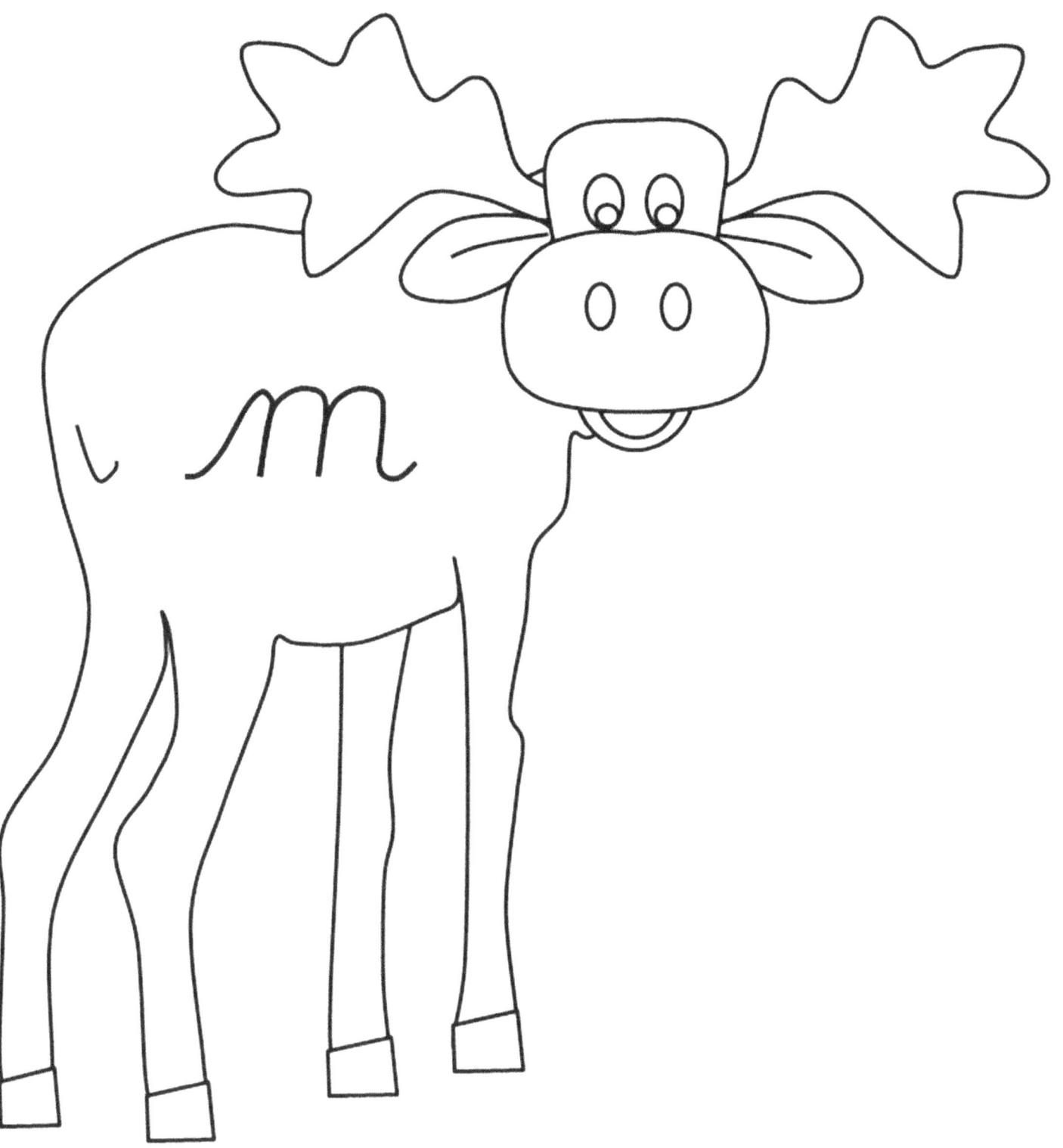

Trace the steps for making the letter m on the following line.

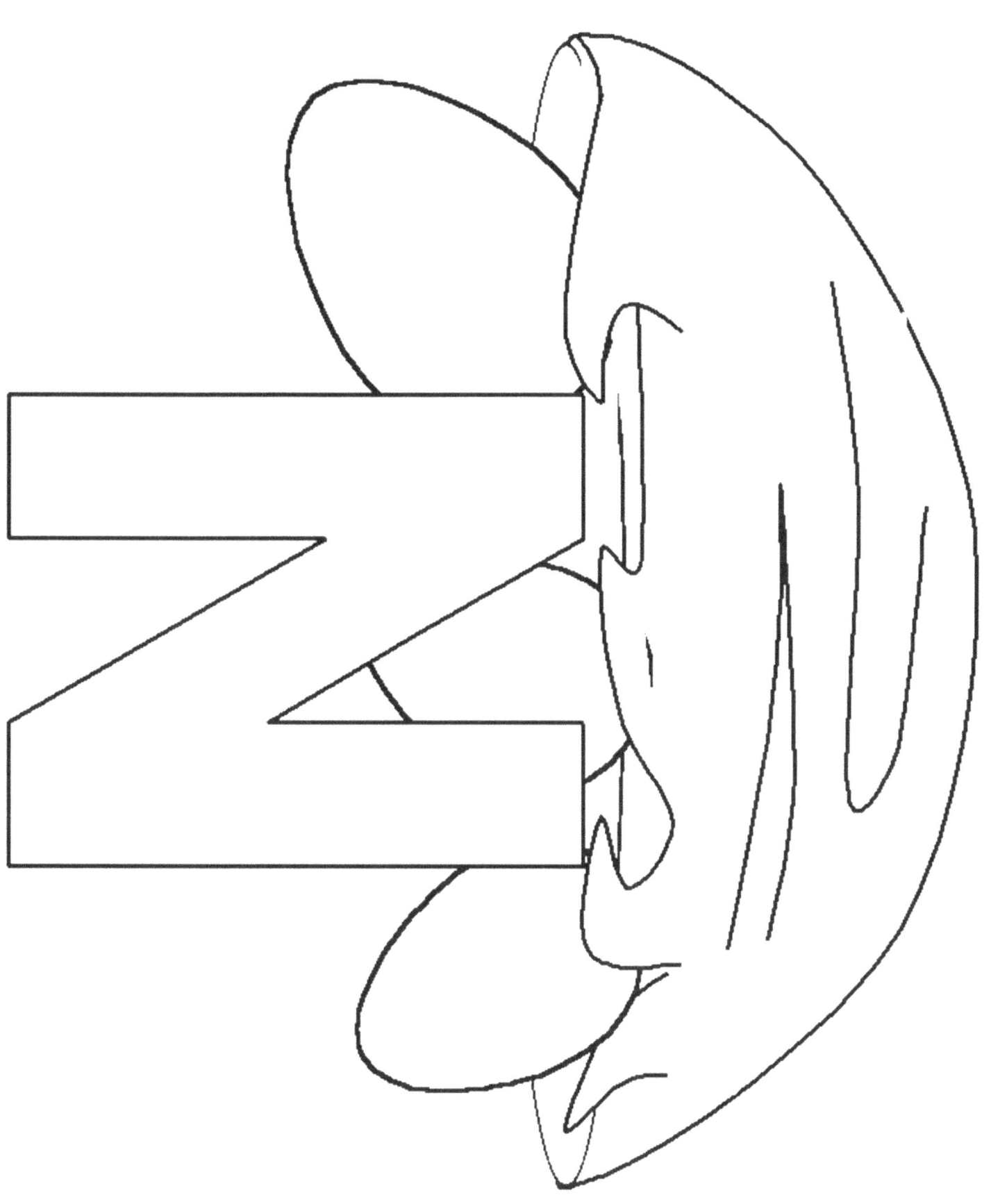

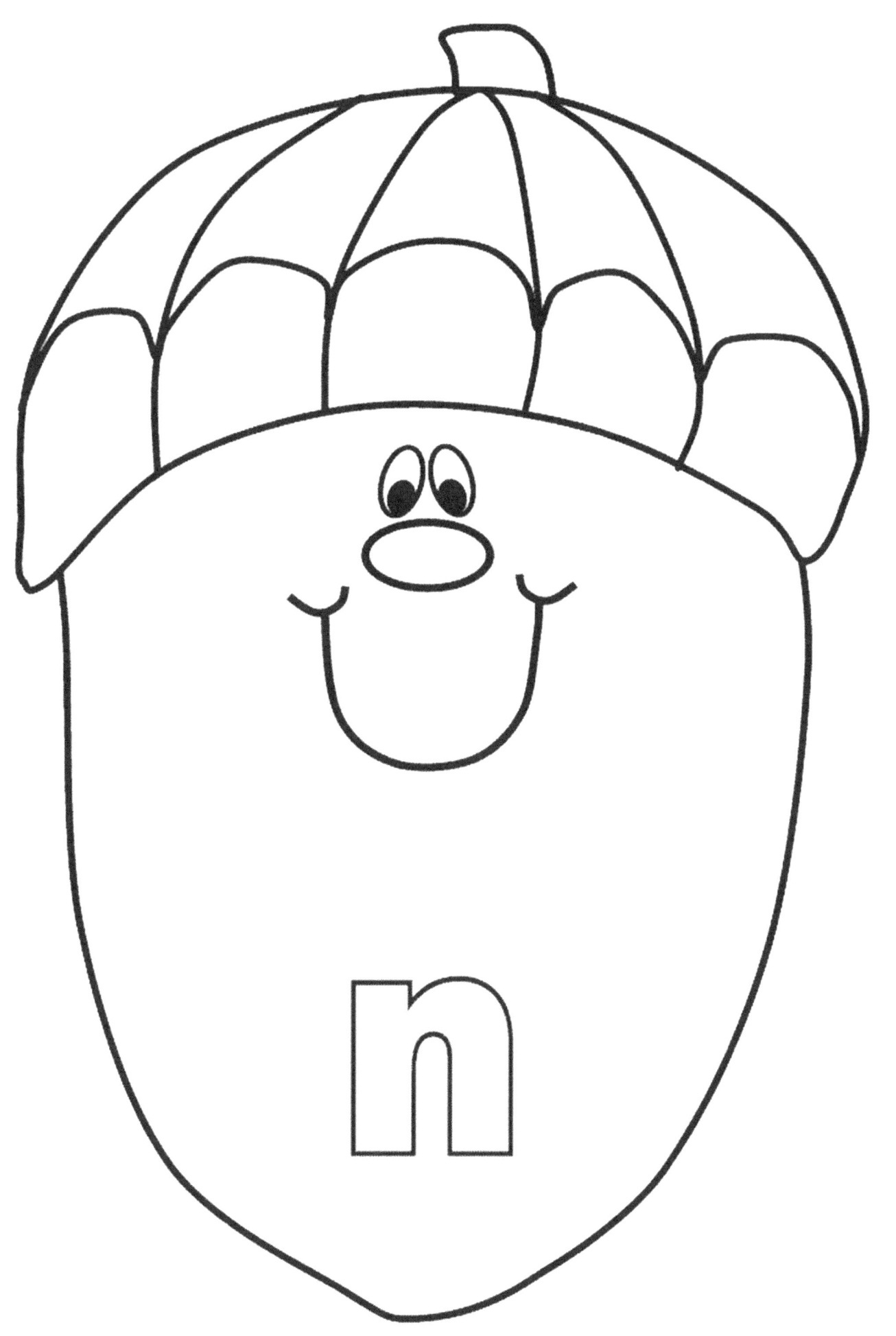

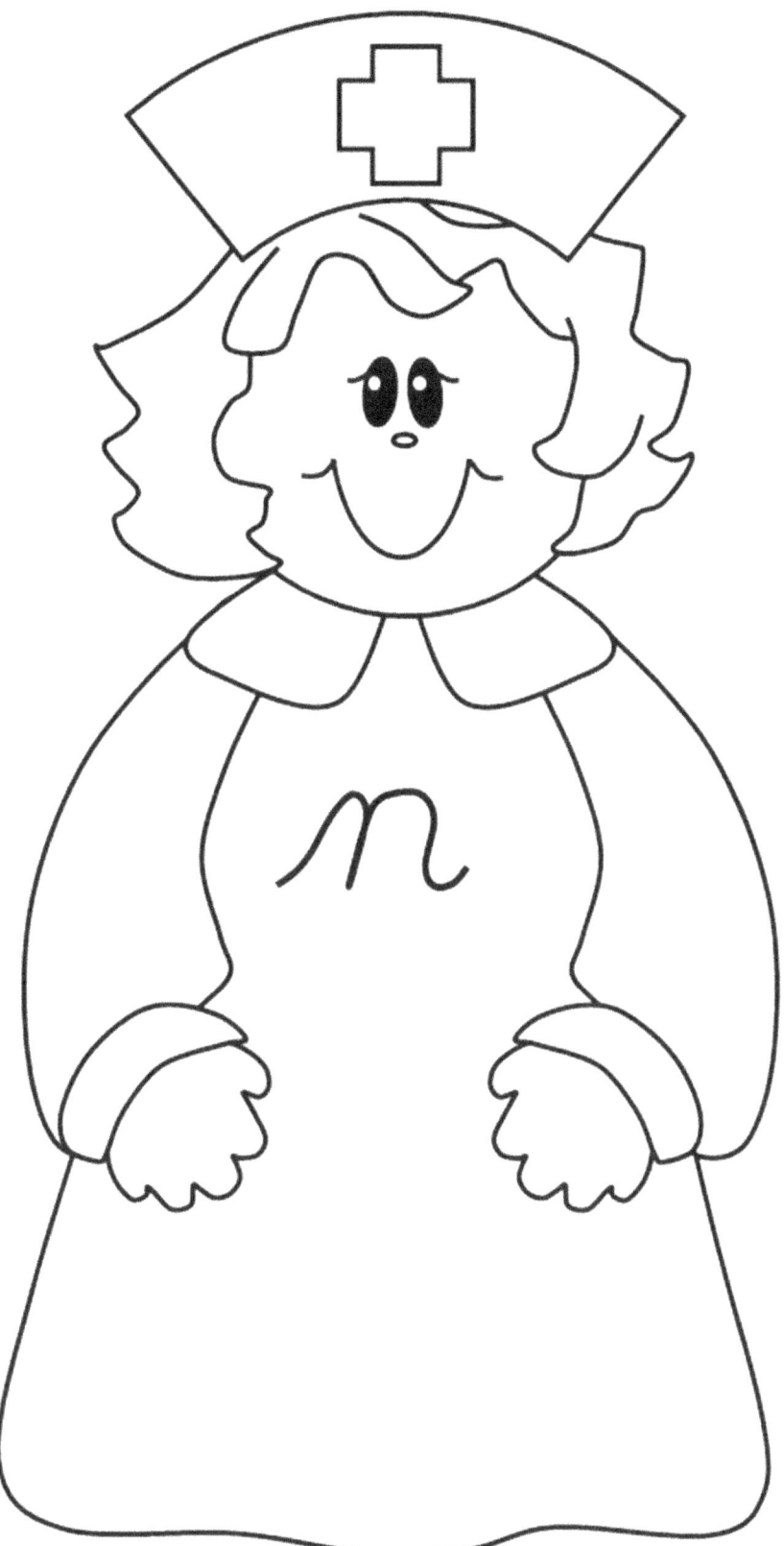

Trace the steps for making the letter n on the following line.

_n   n   n   n   n   n   n   nn_

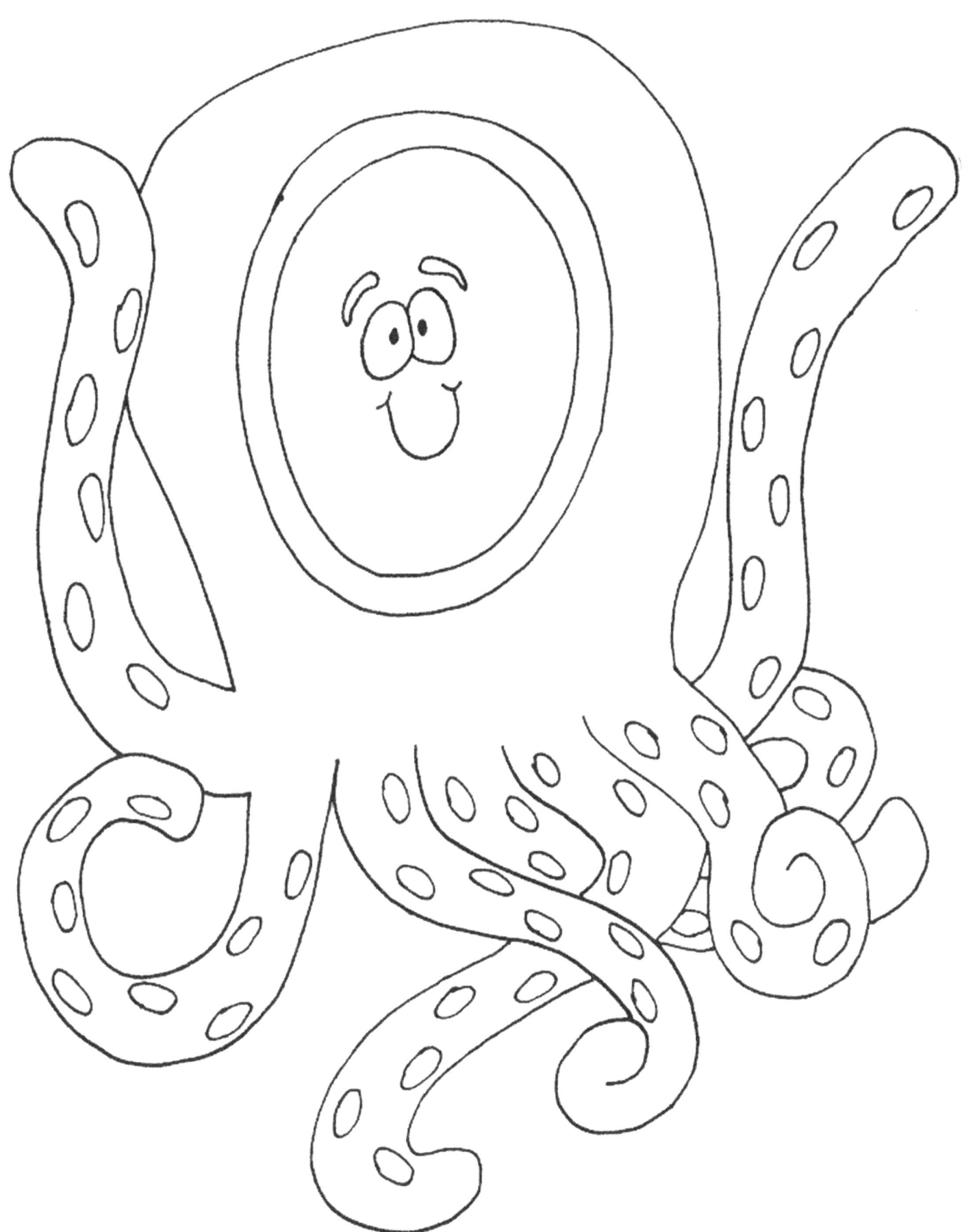

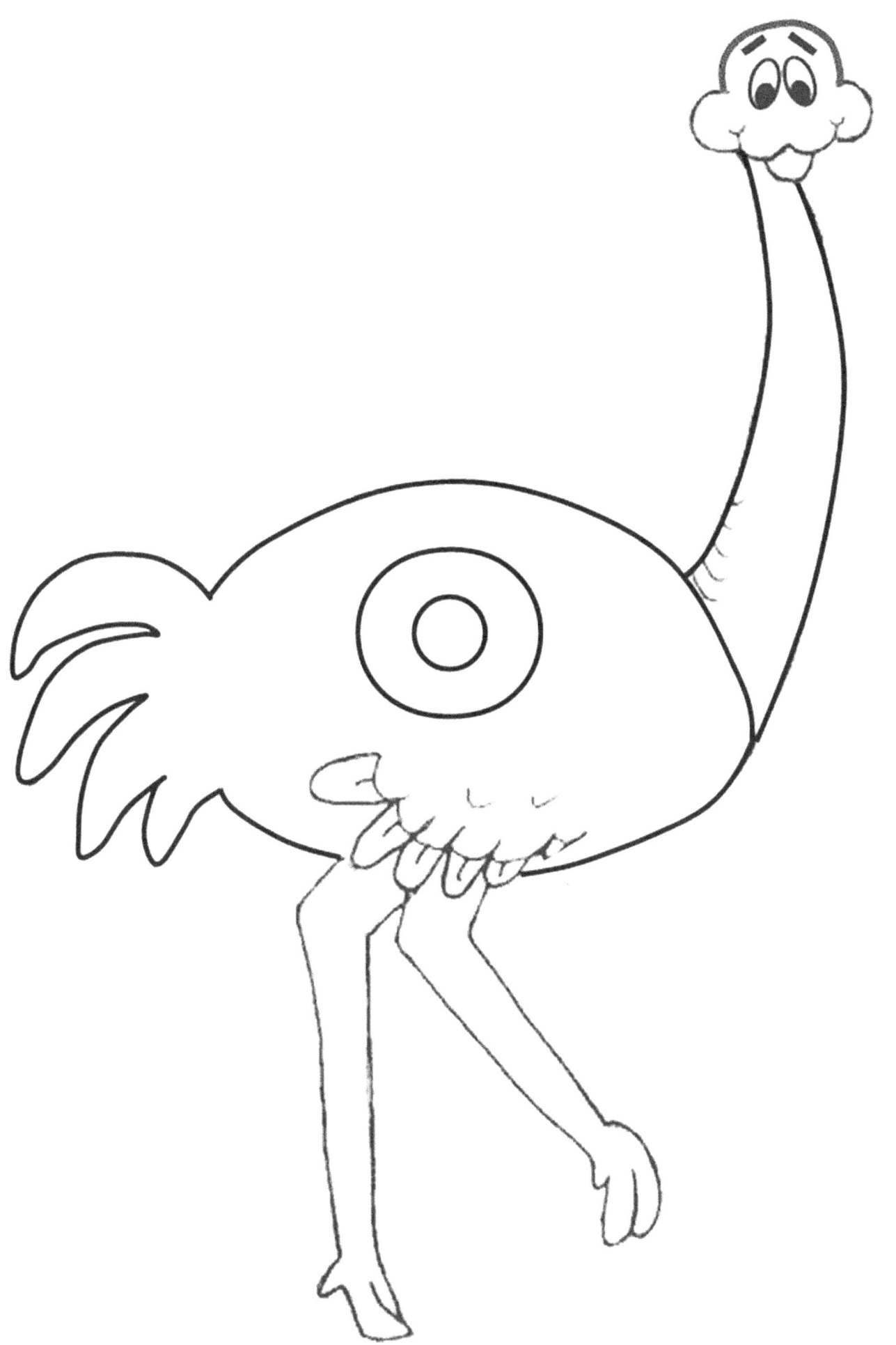

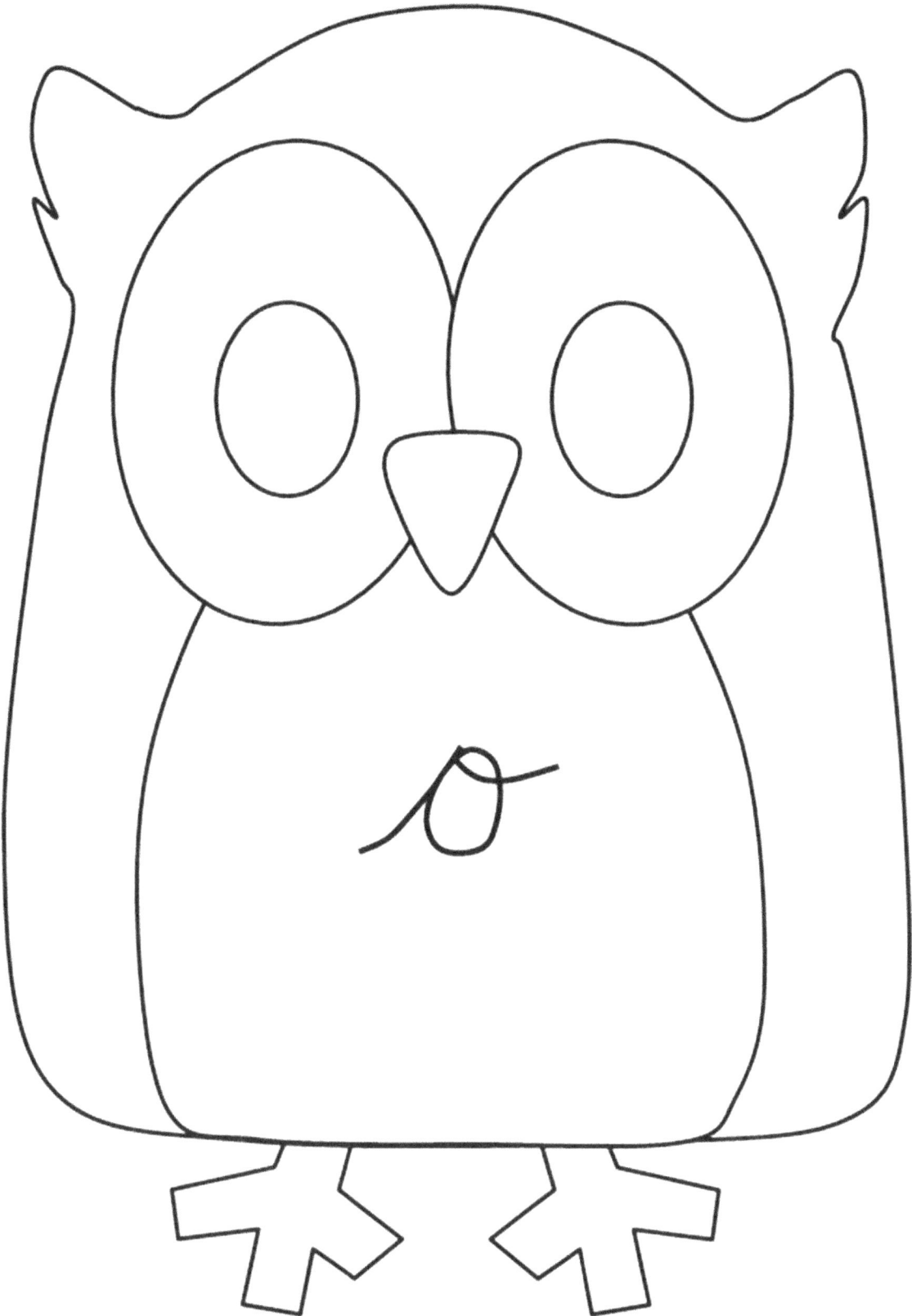

Trace the steps for making the letter o on the following line.

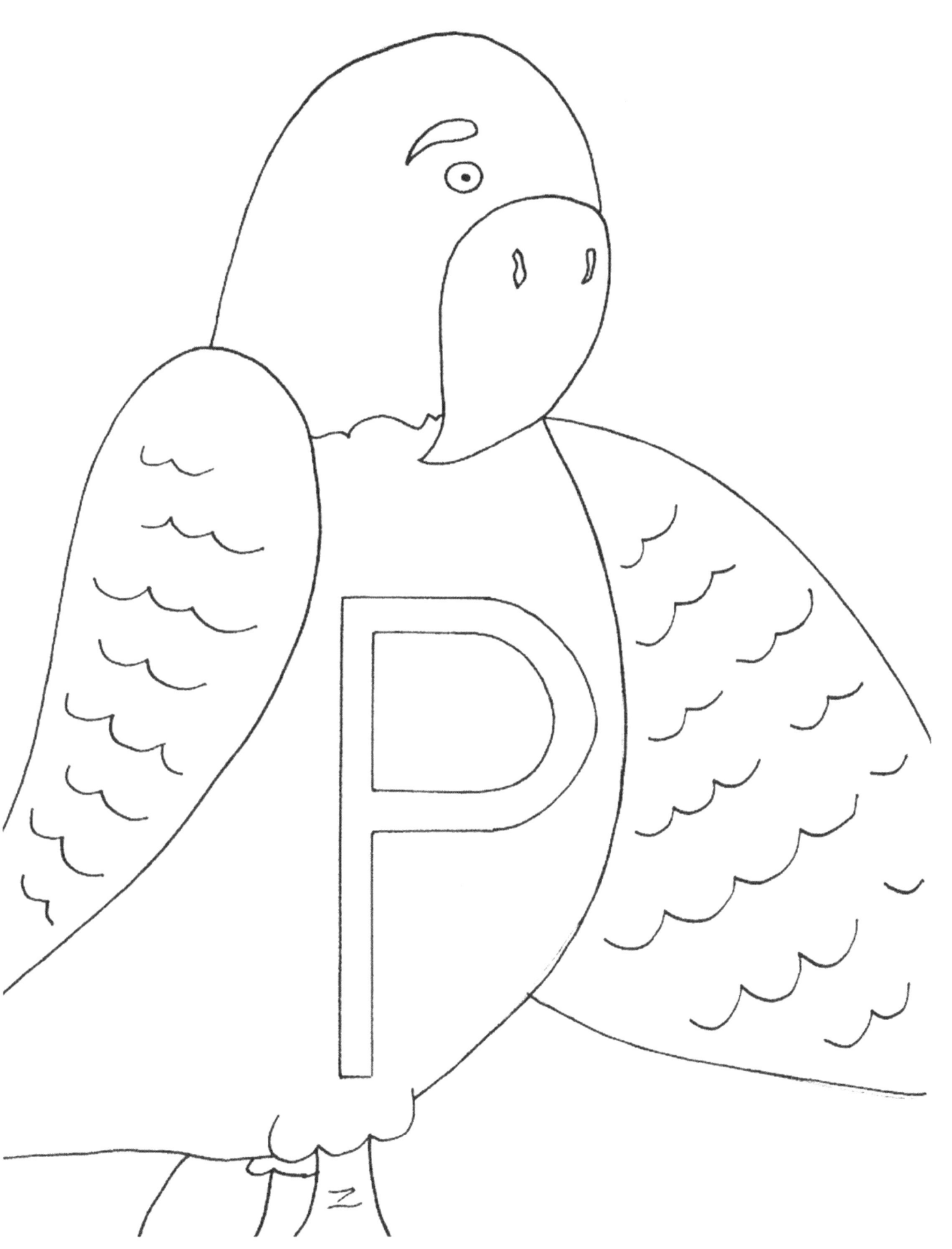

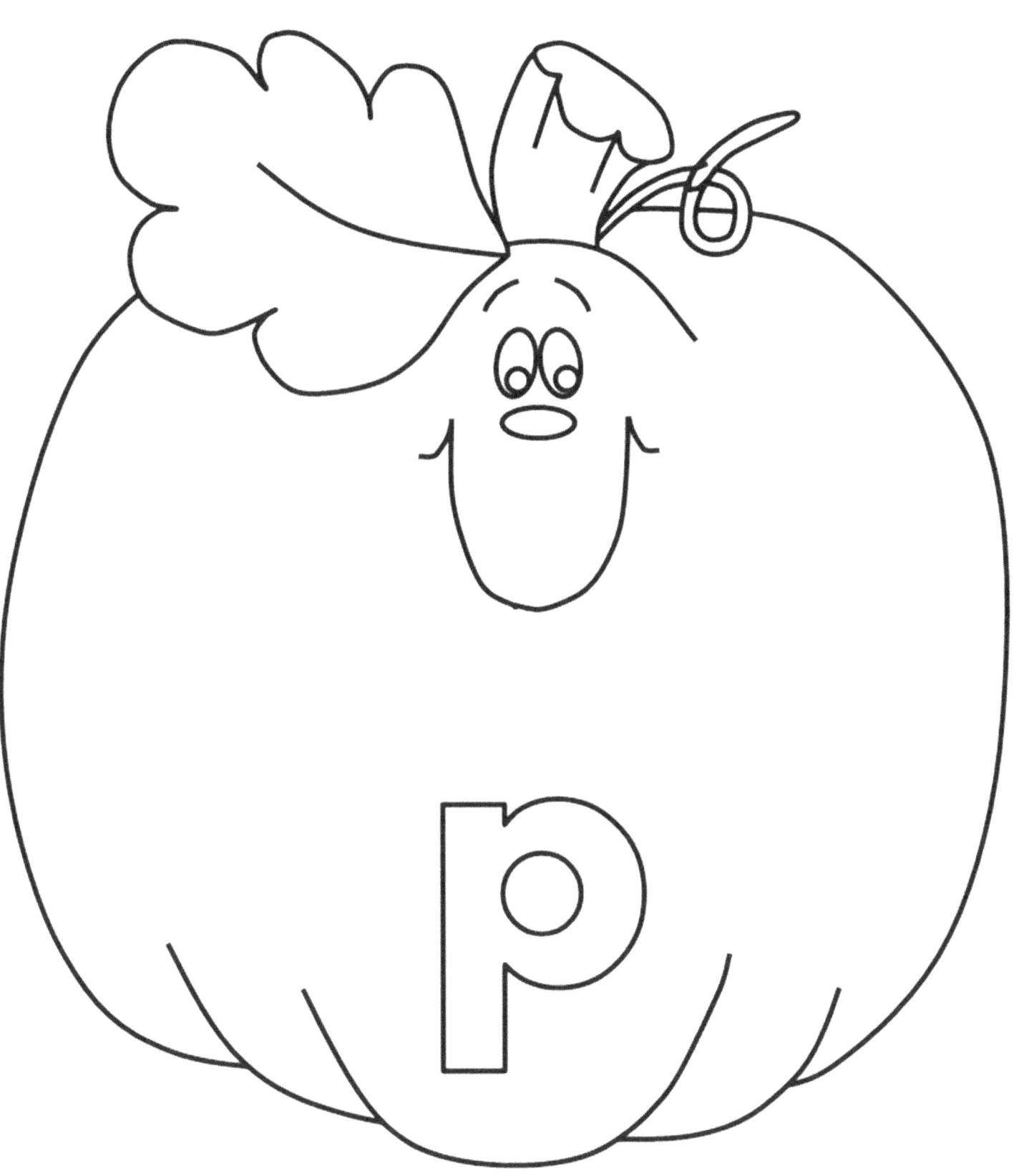

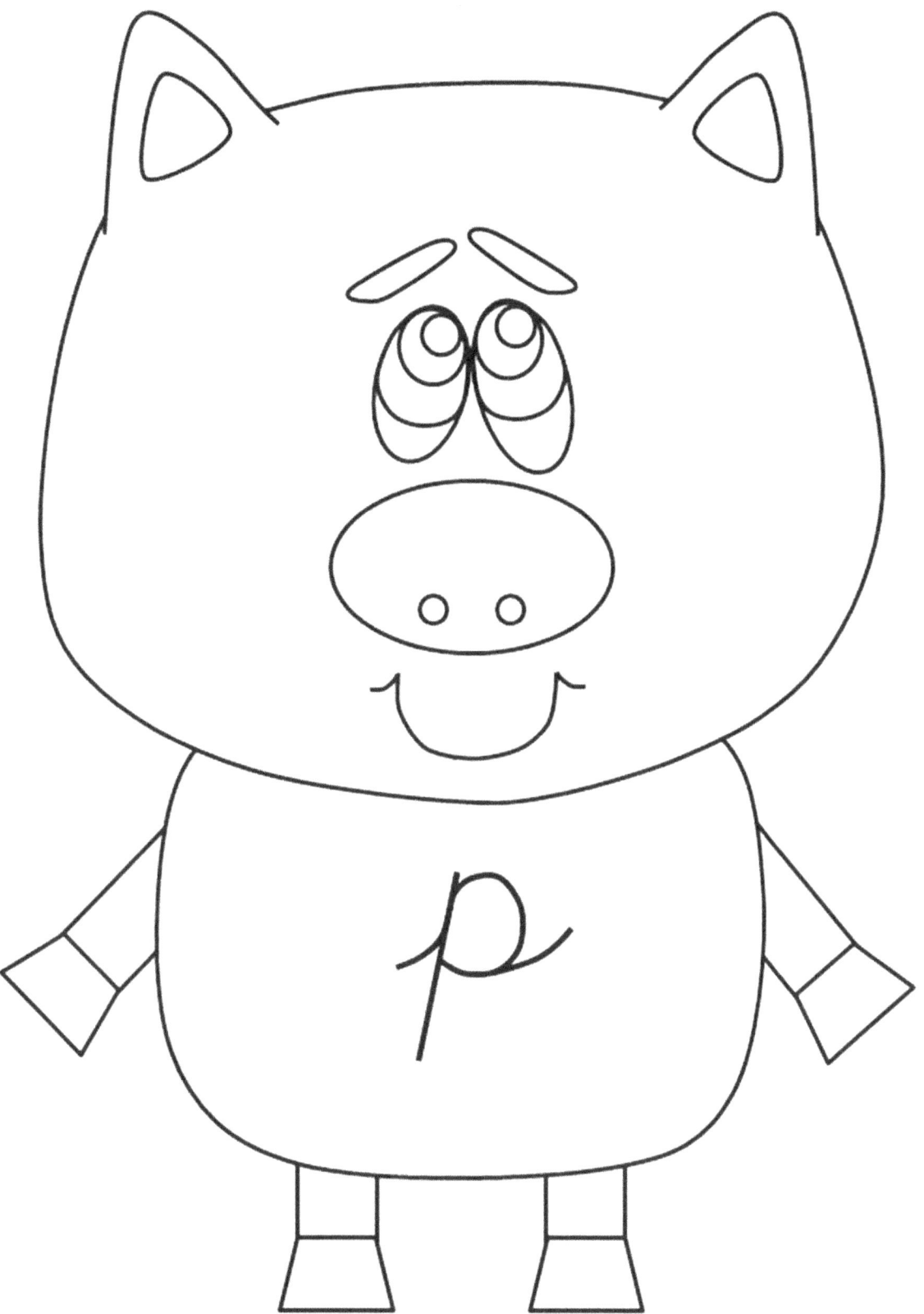

Trace the steps for making the letter p on the following line.

p   p   p   p   pp

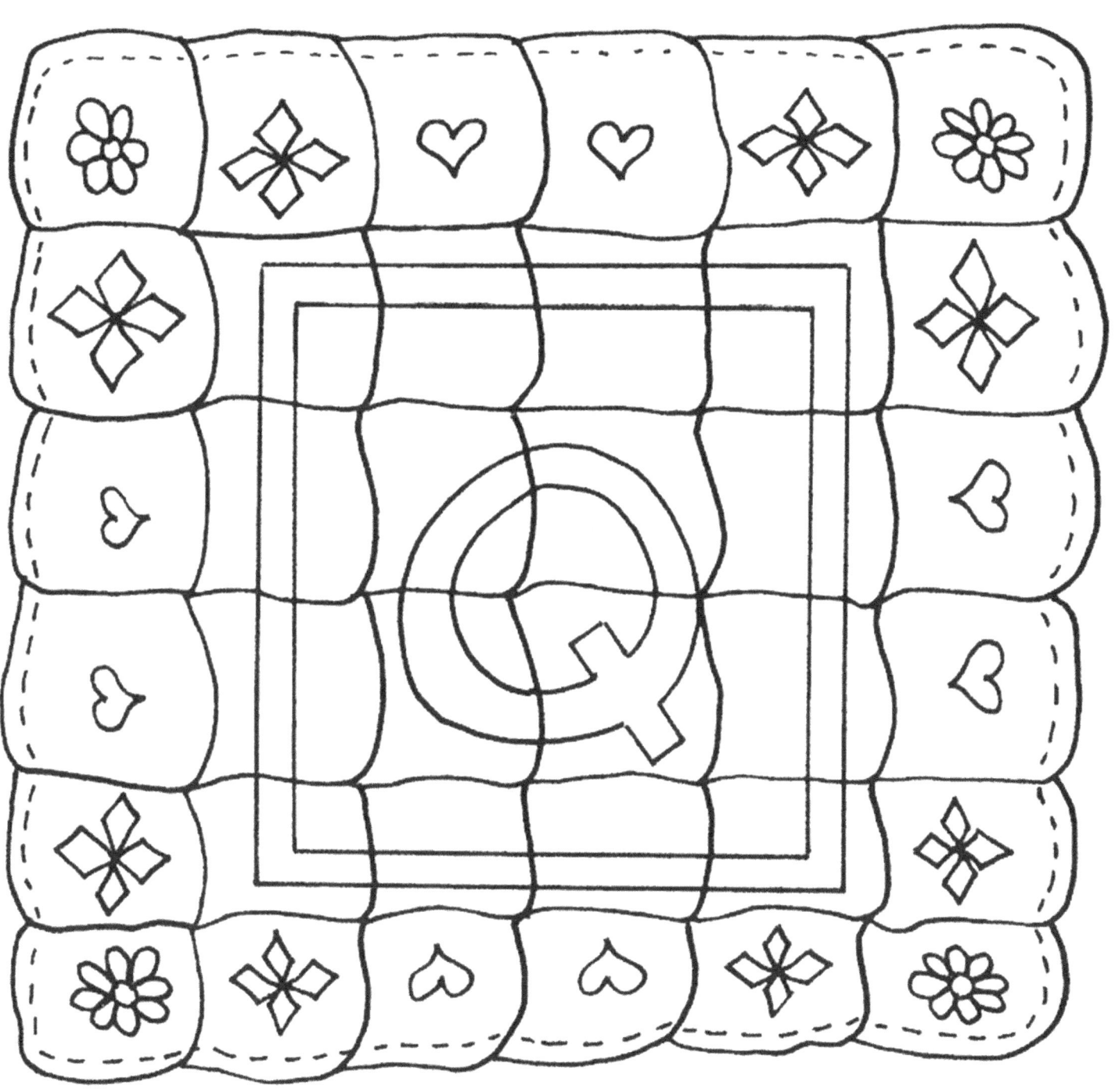

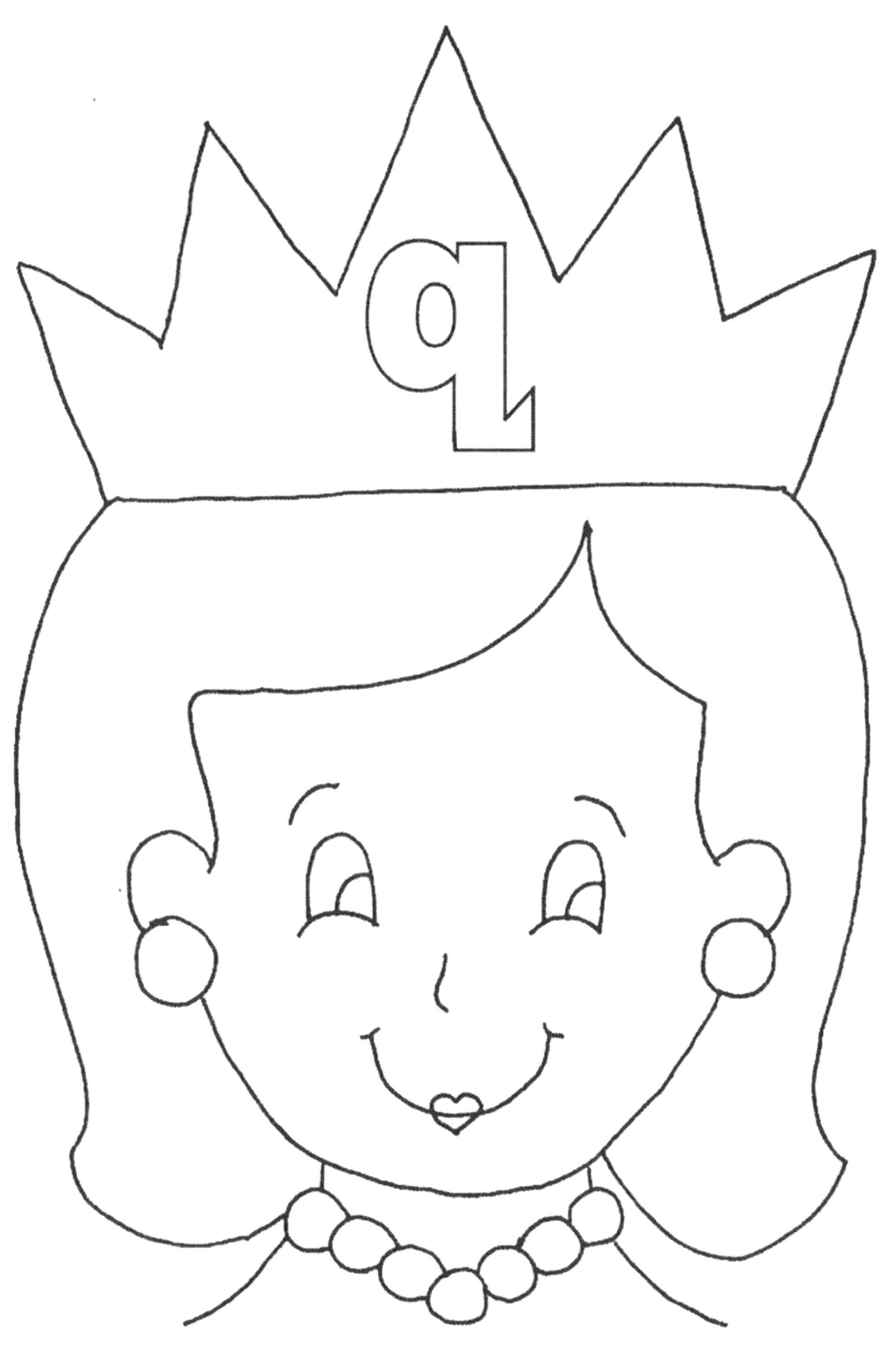

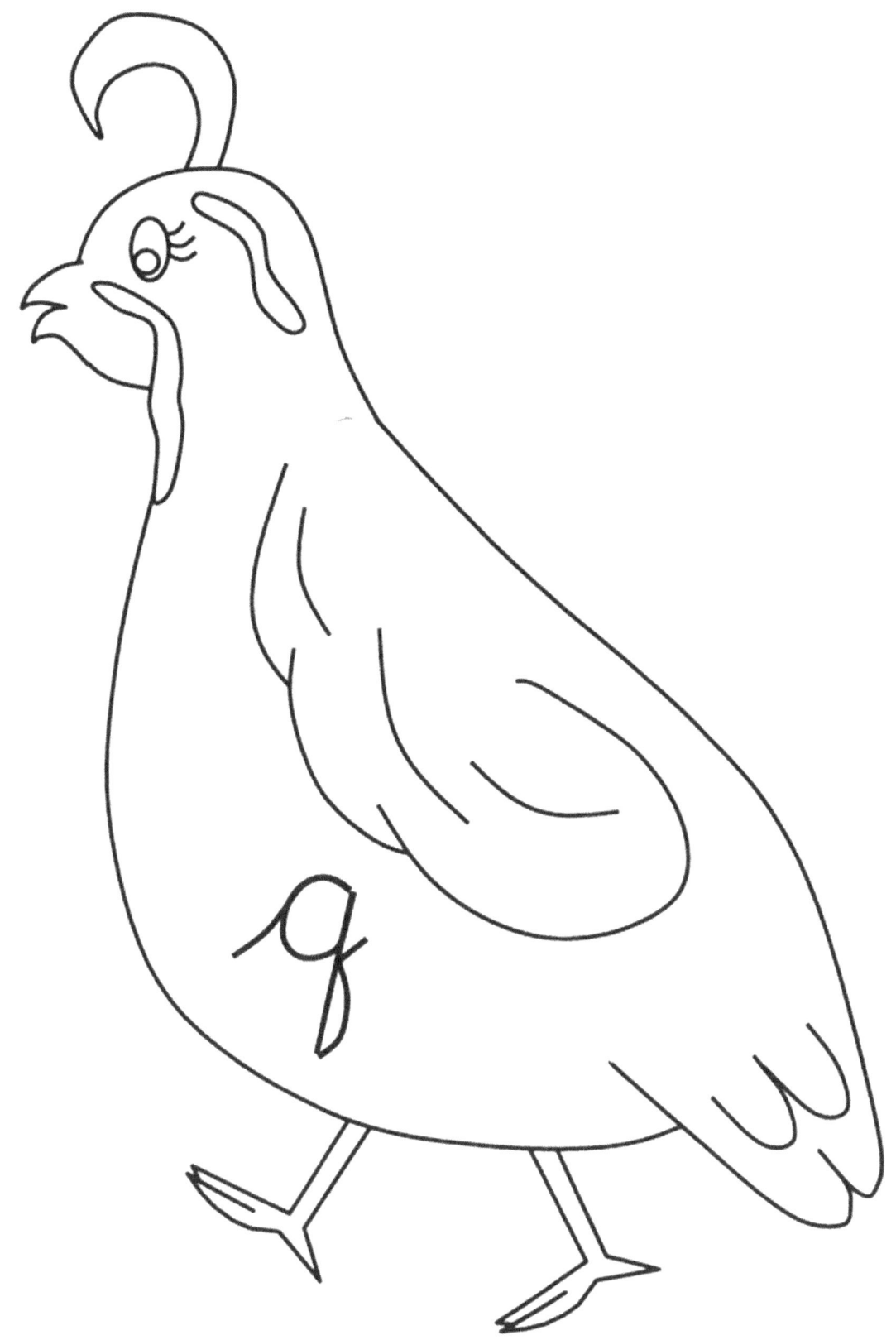

Trace the steps for making the letter q on the following line.

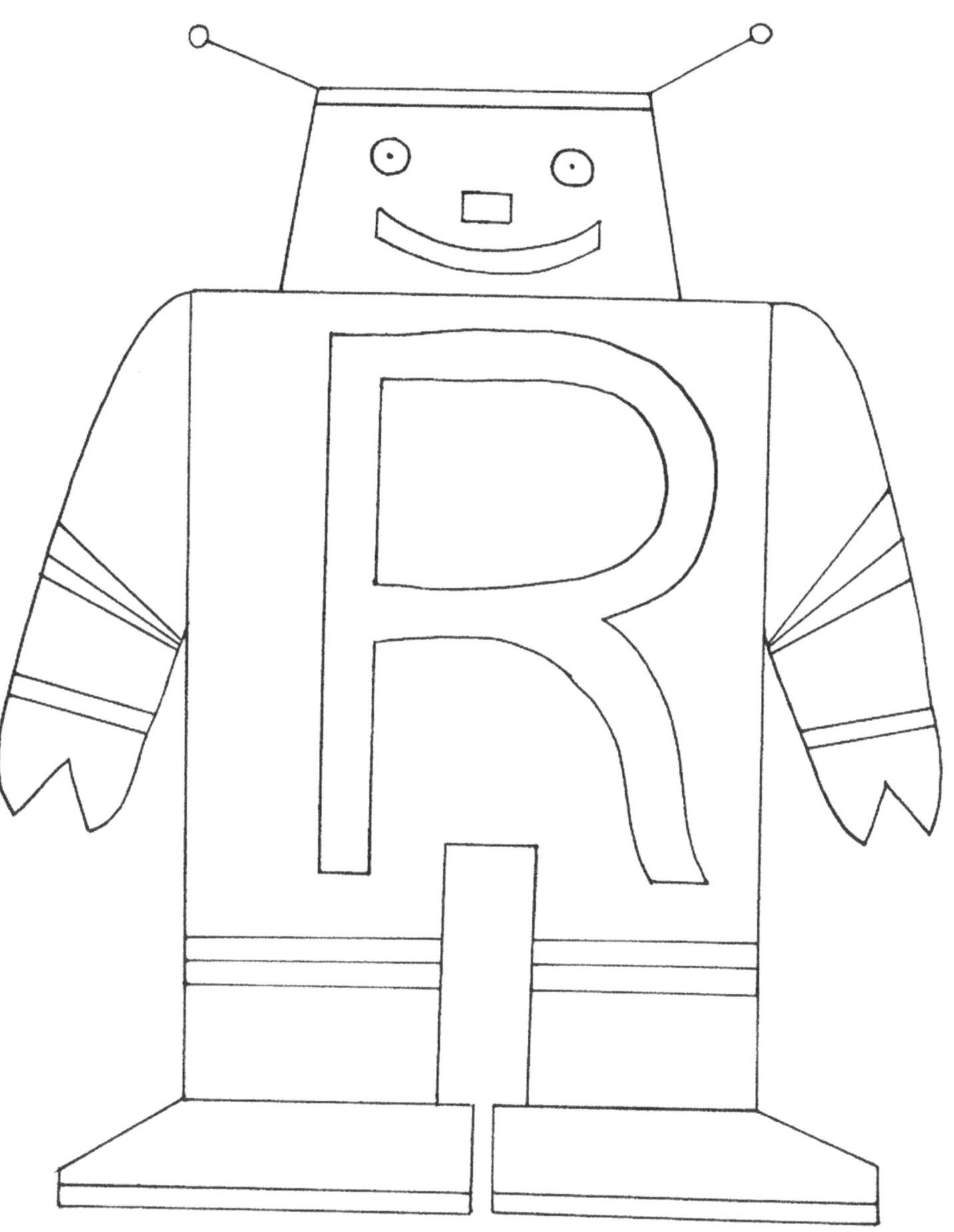

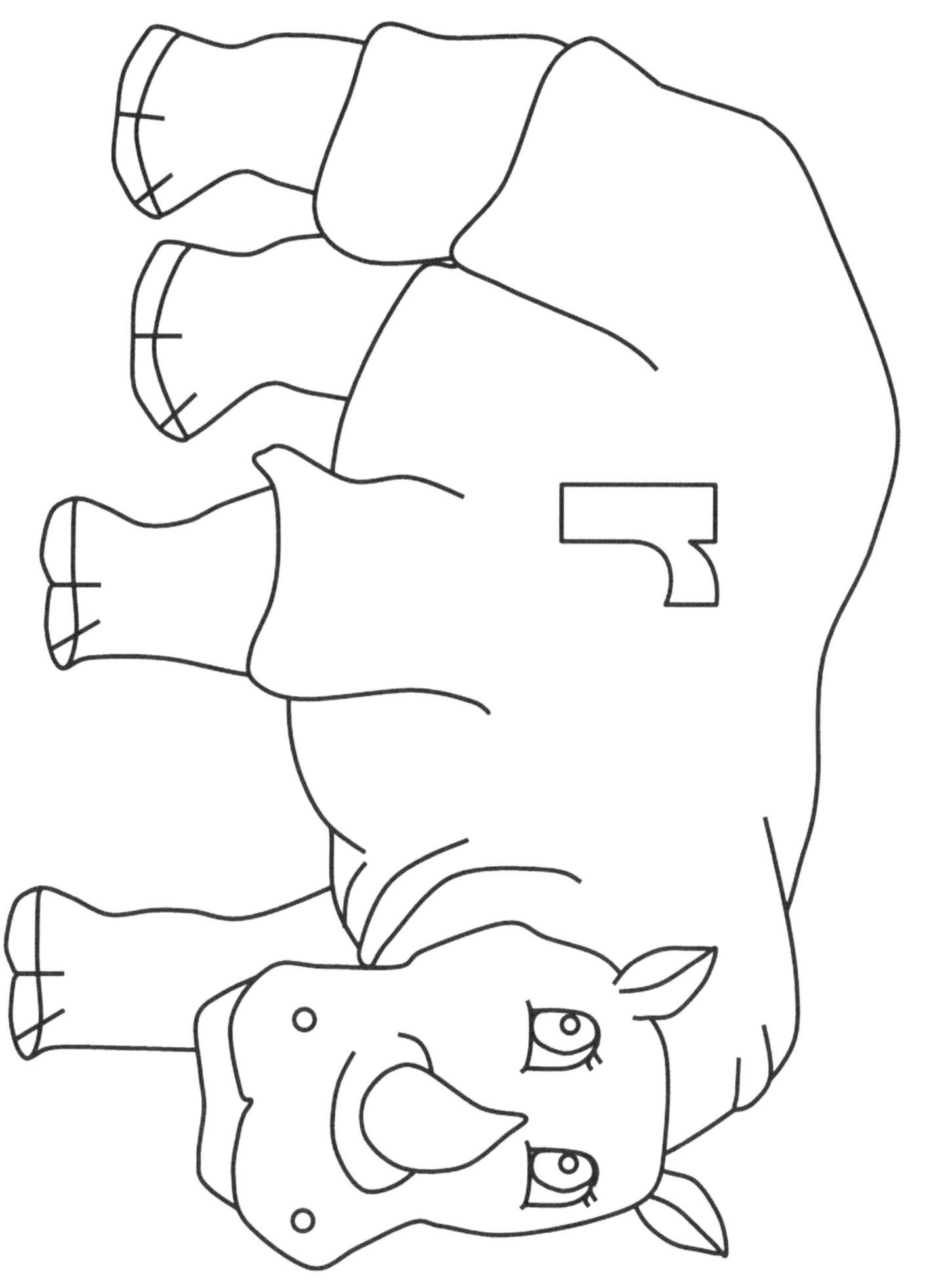

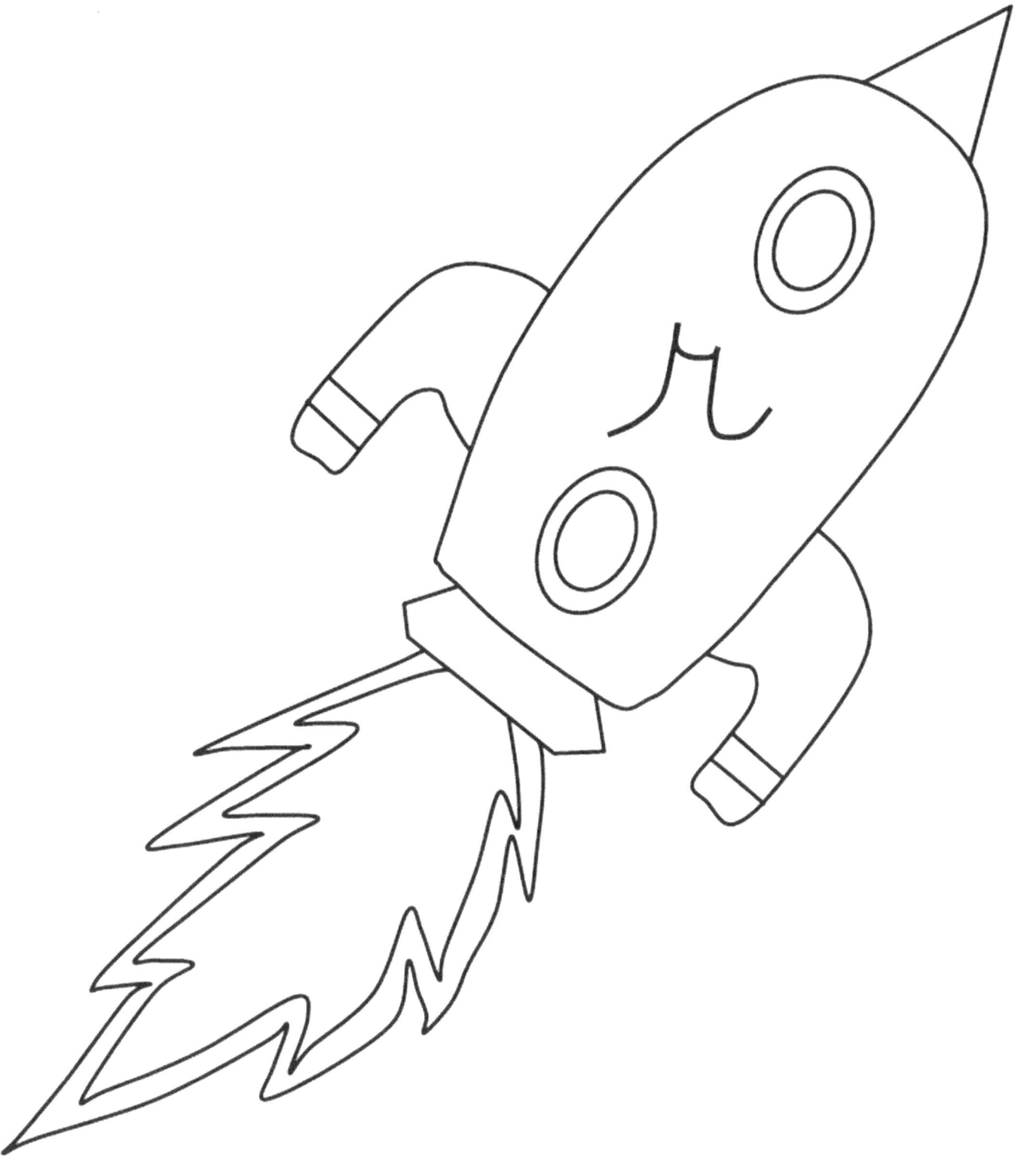

Trace the steps for making the letter r on the following line.

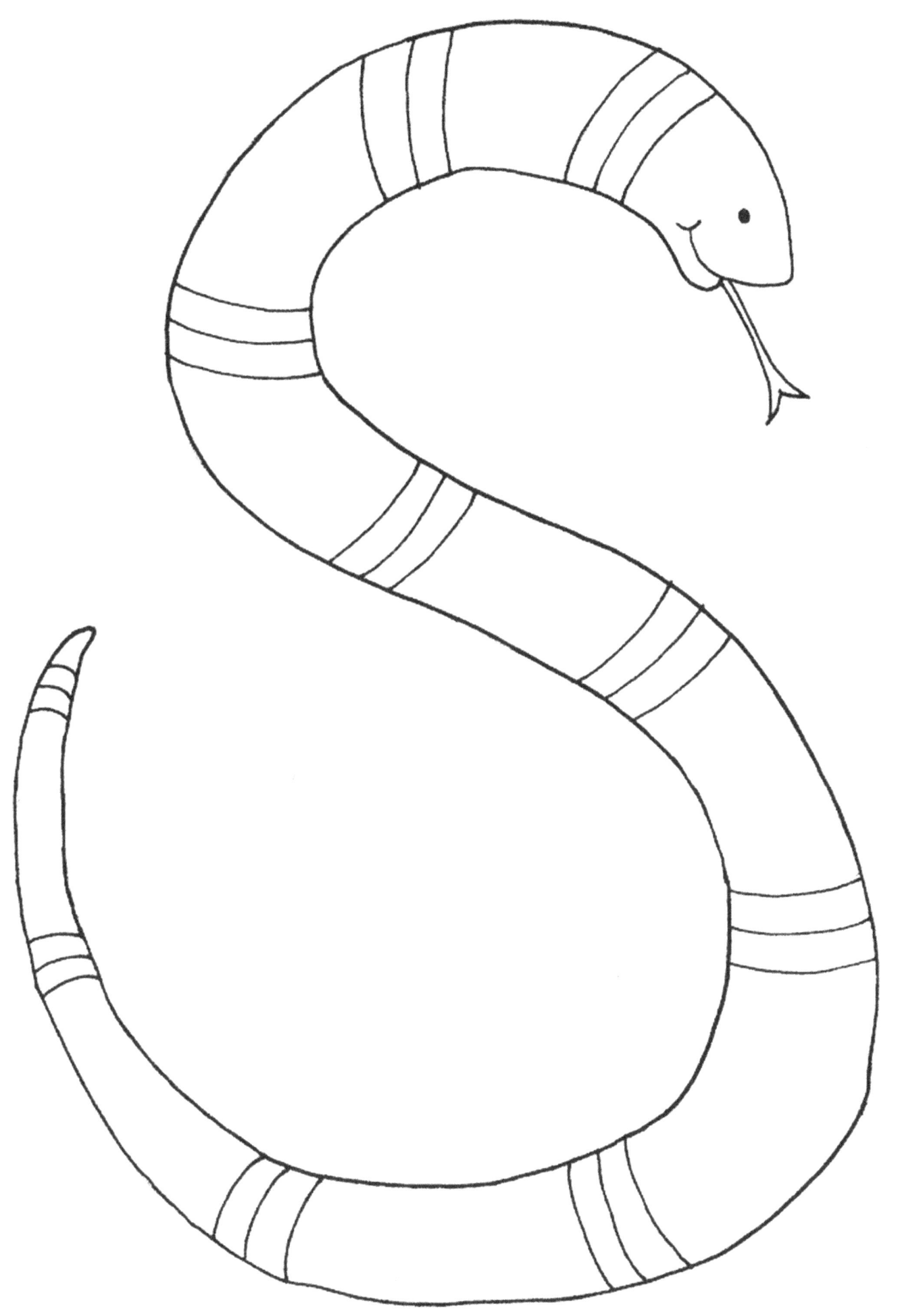

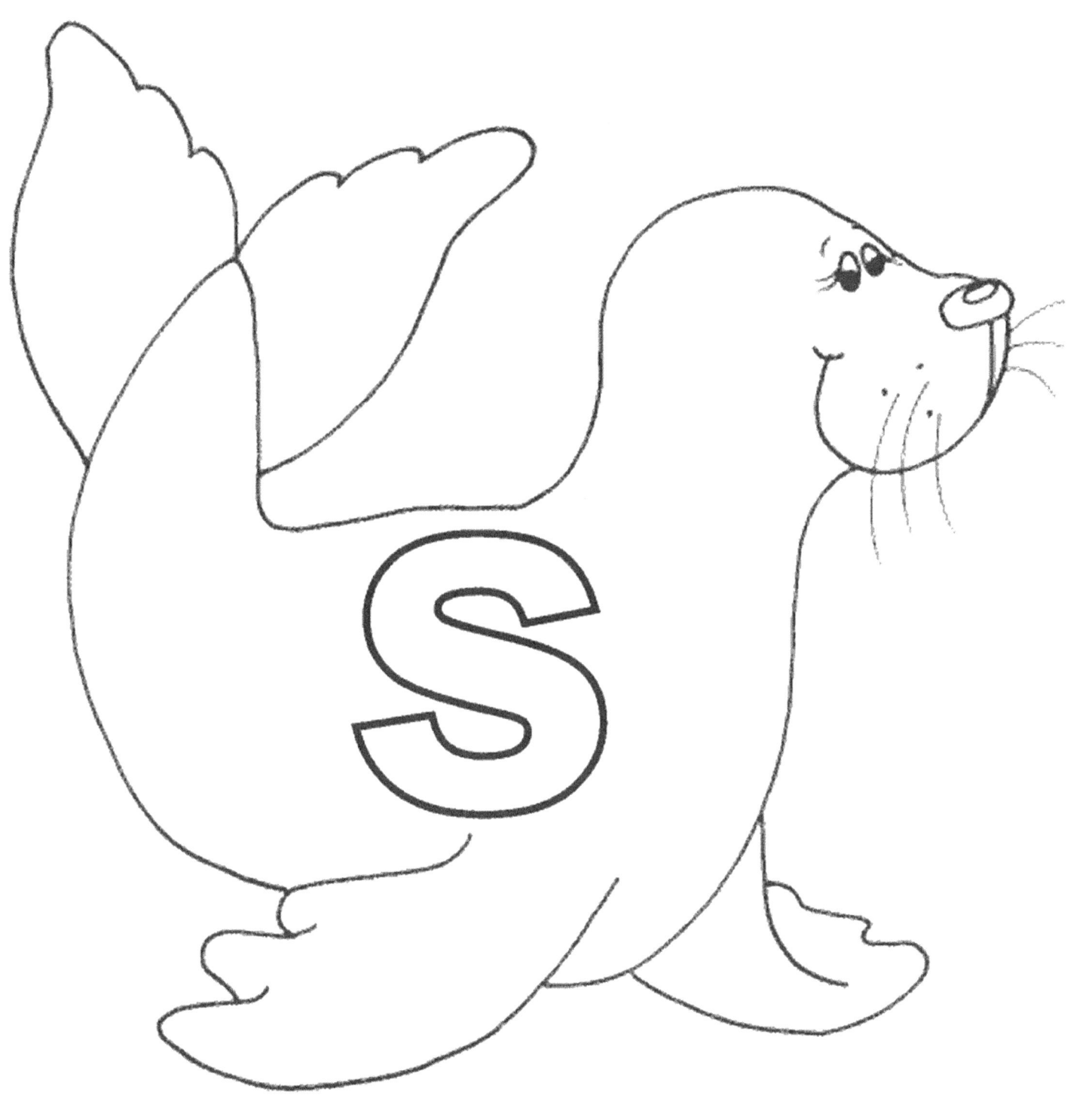

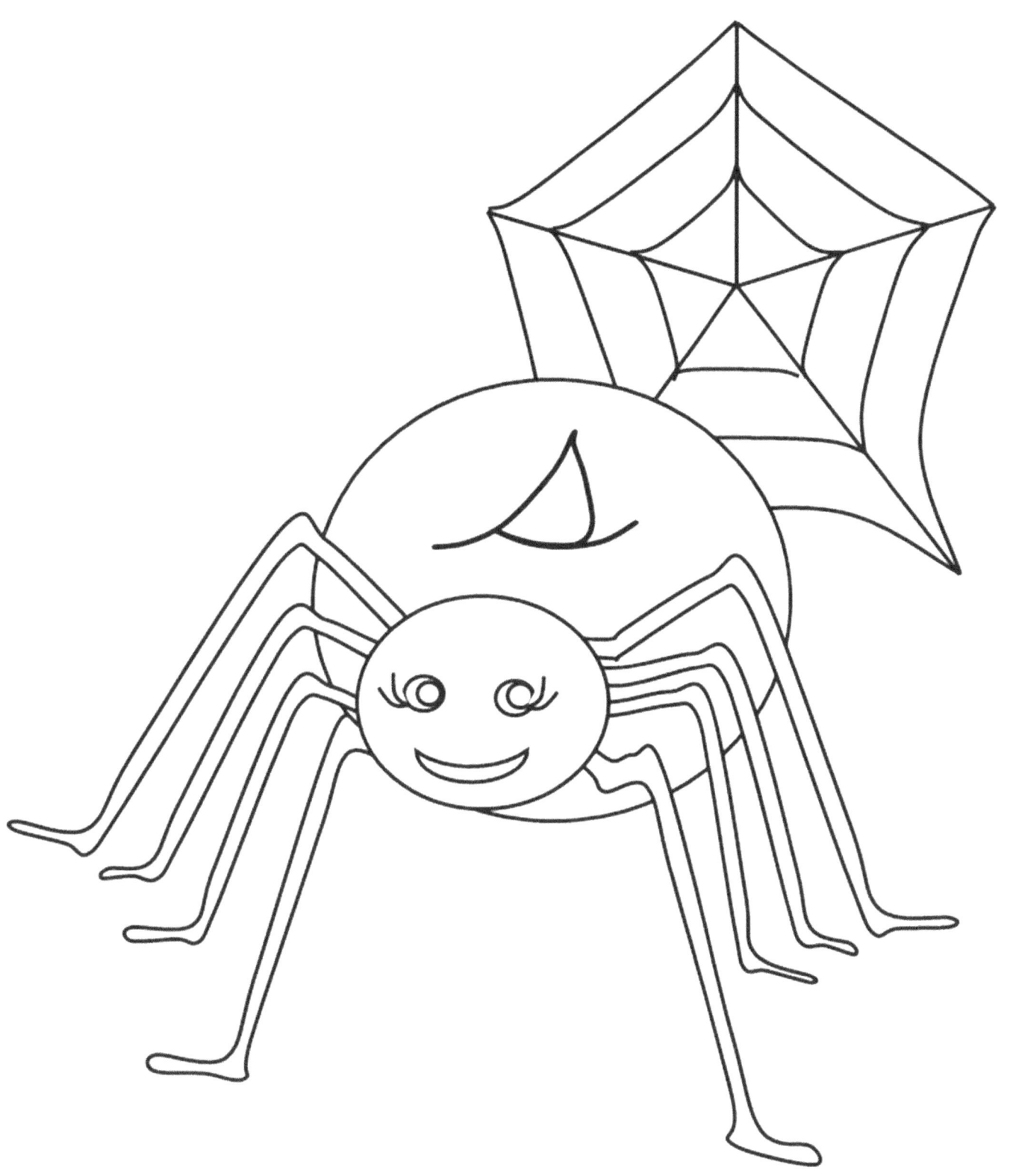

Trace the steps for making the letter s on the following line.

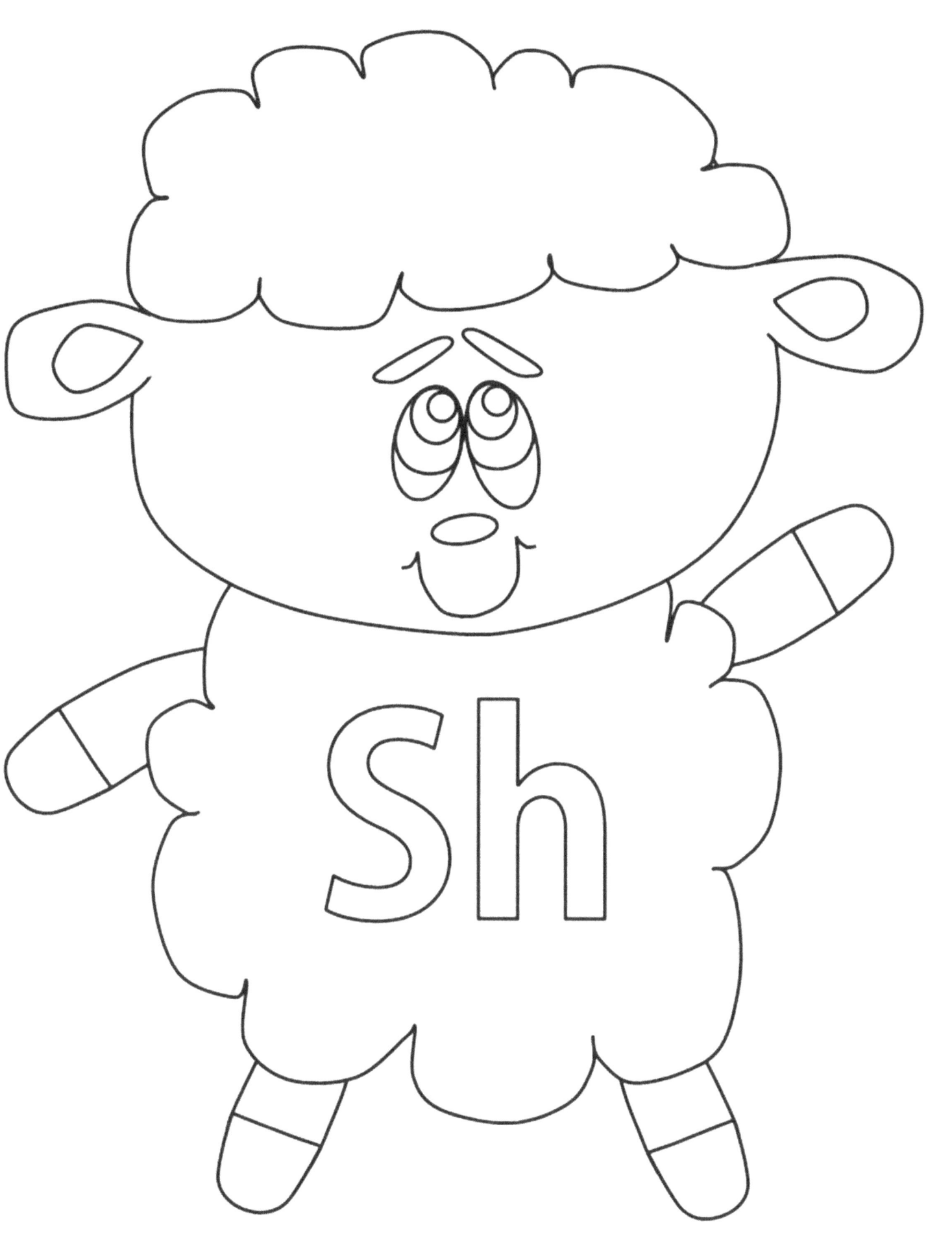

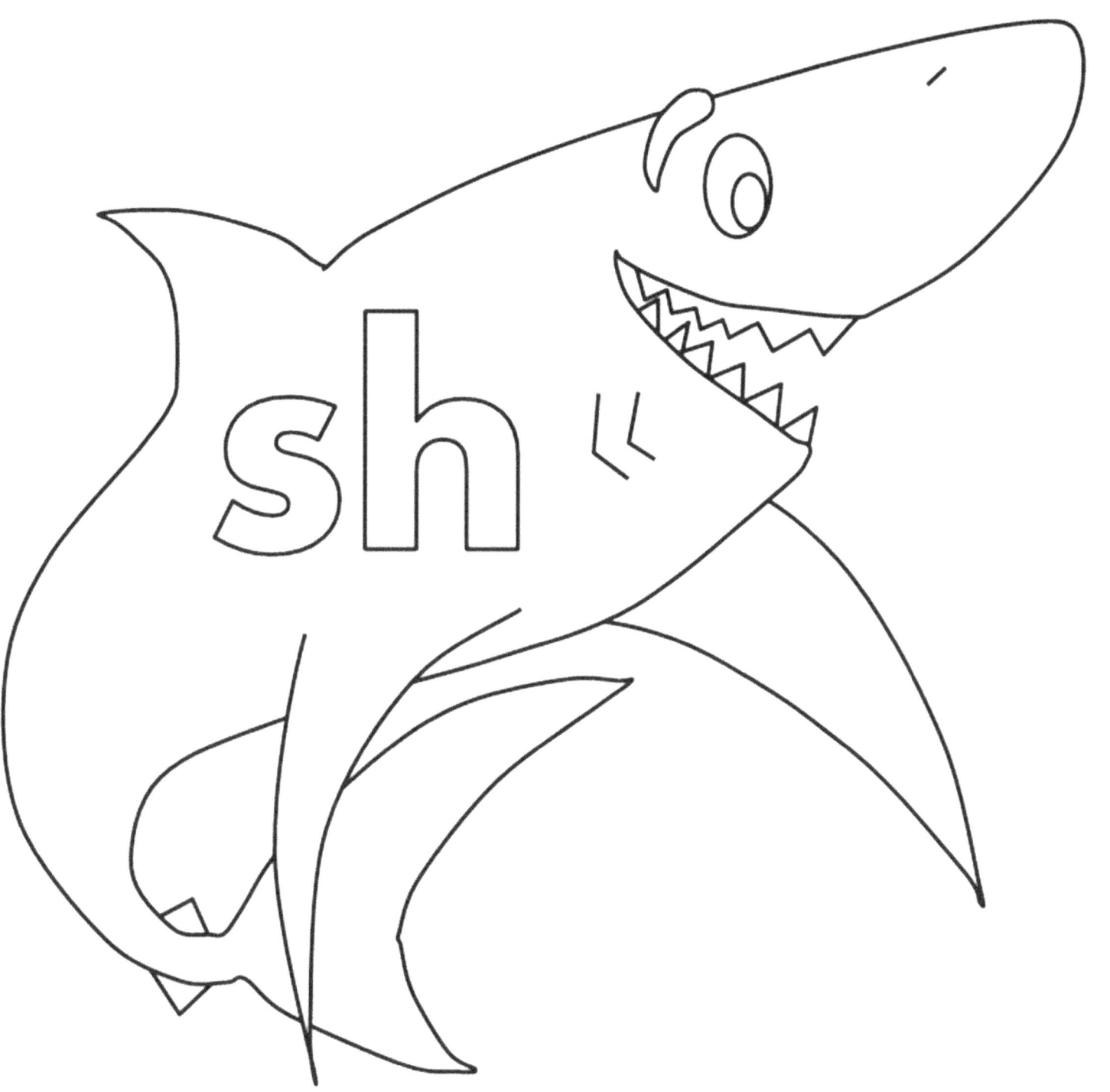

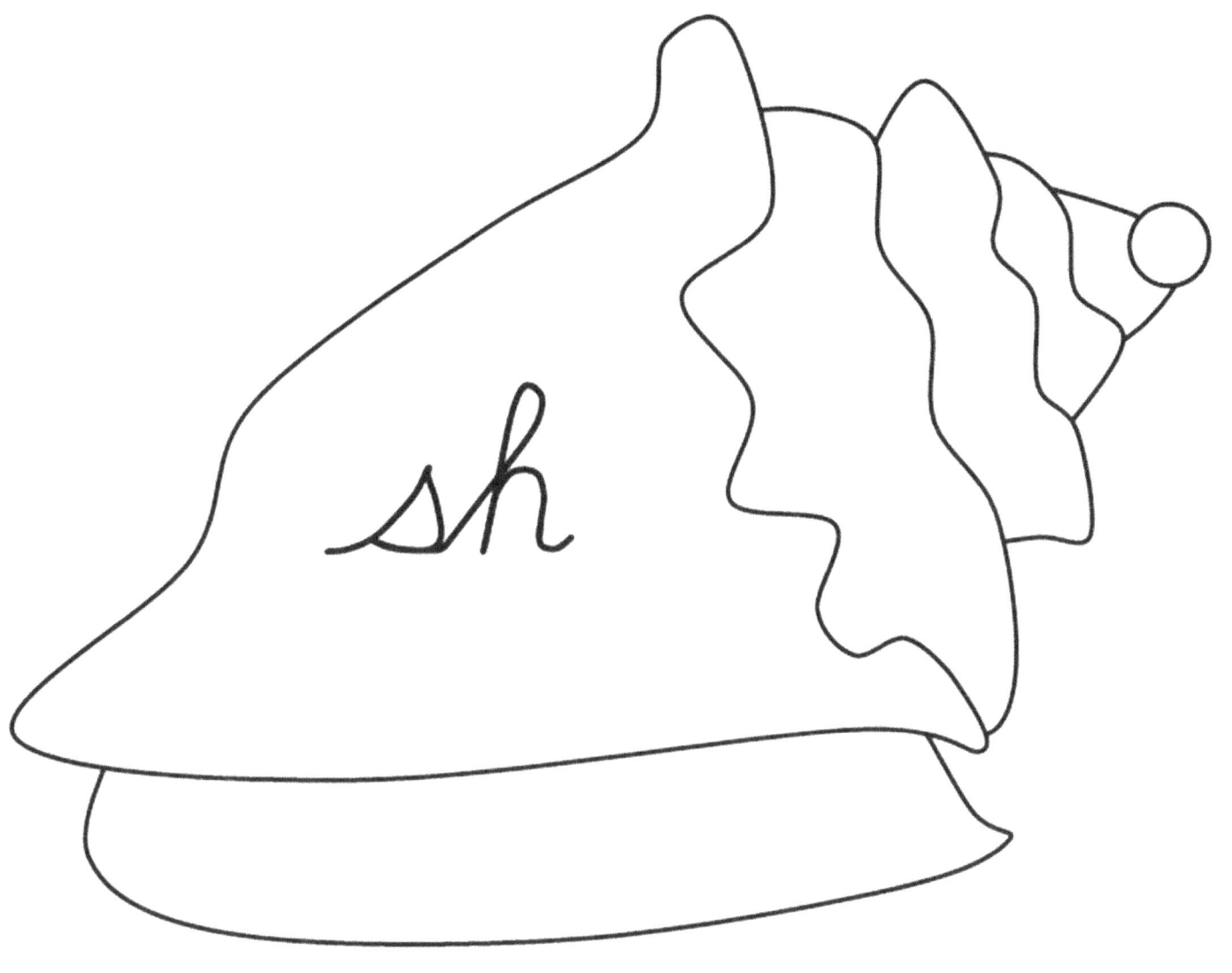

Trace the steps for making the letter sh on the following line.

sh   sh   sh   sh   sh

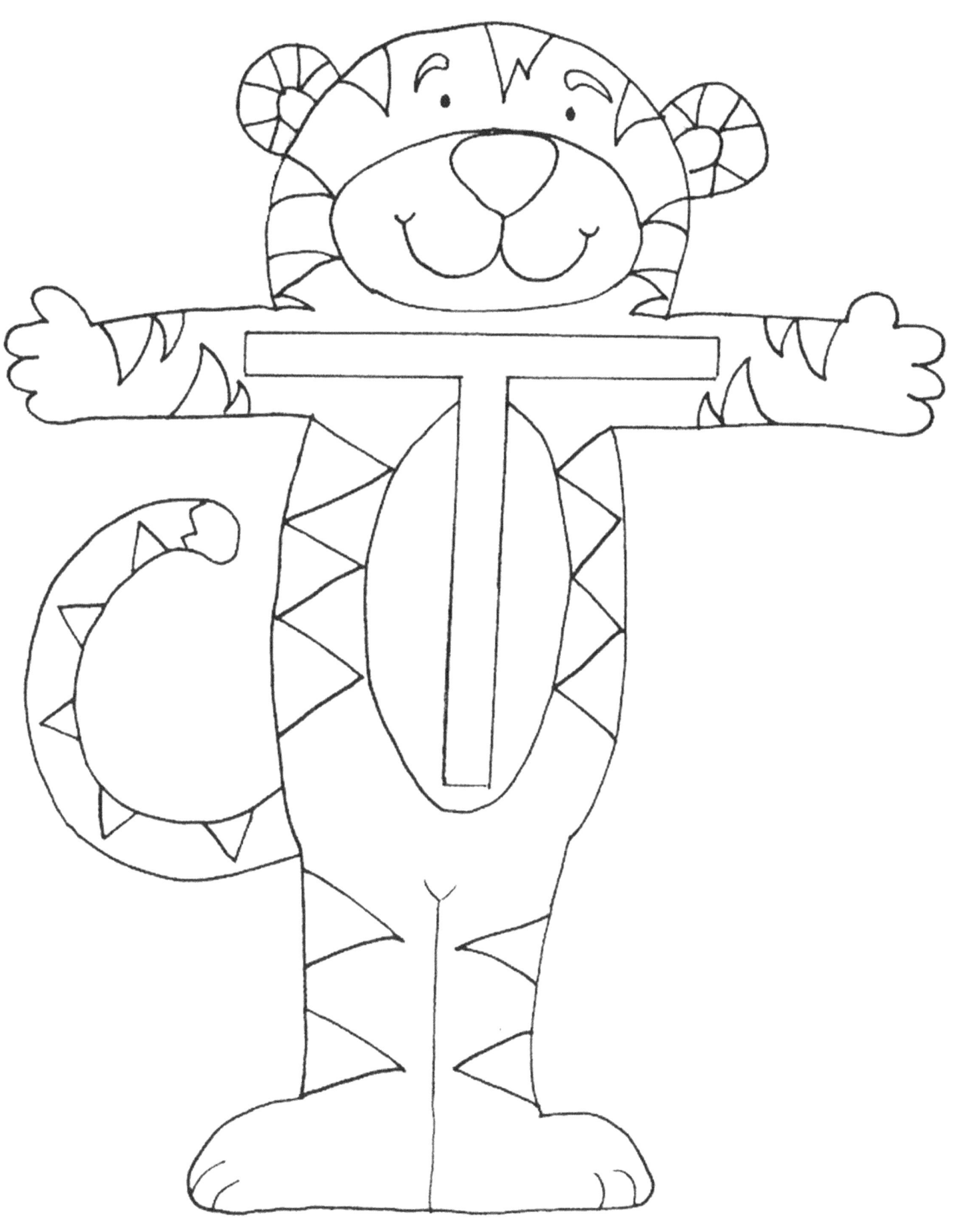

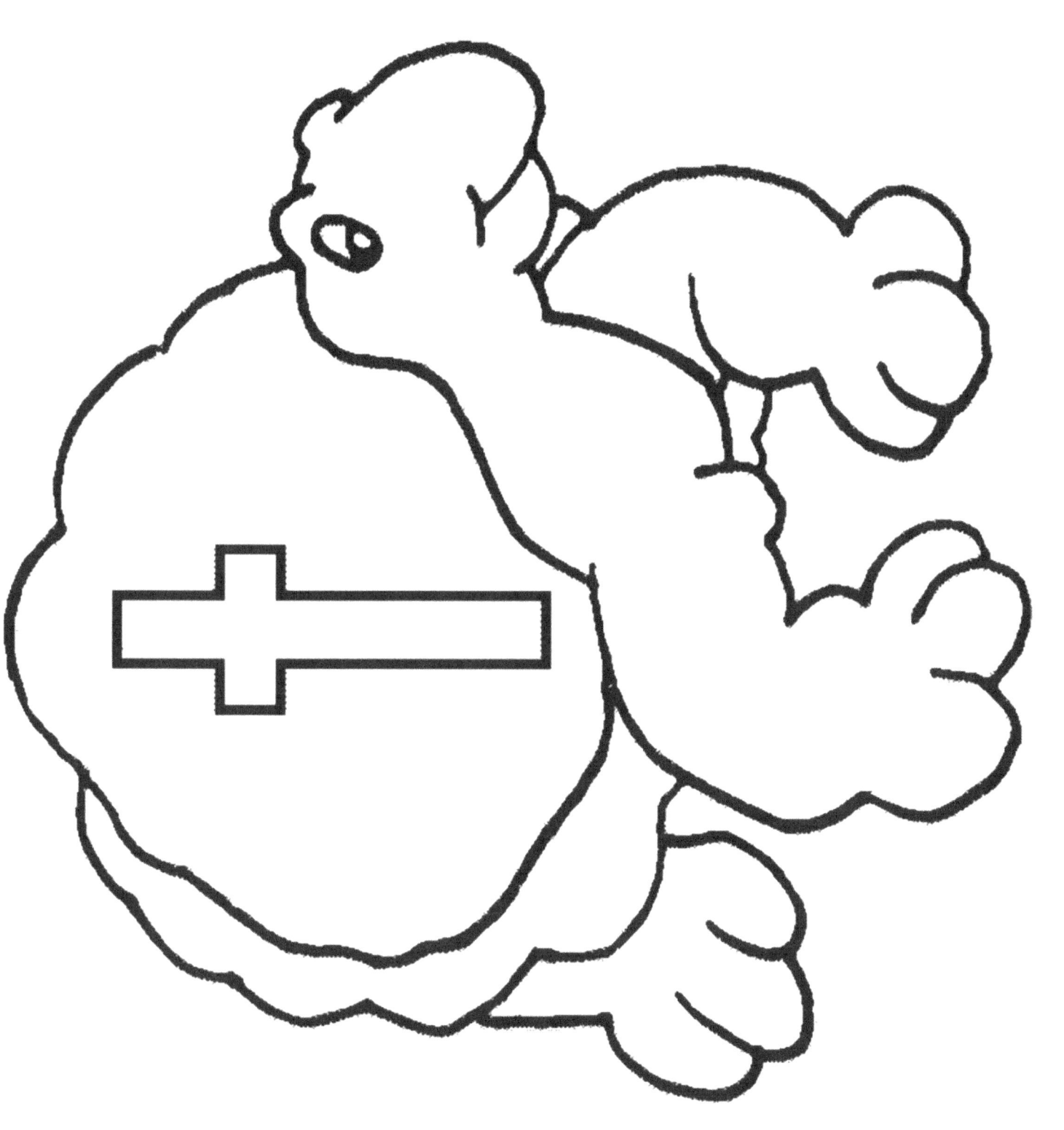

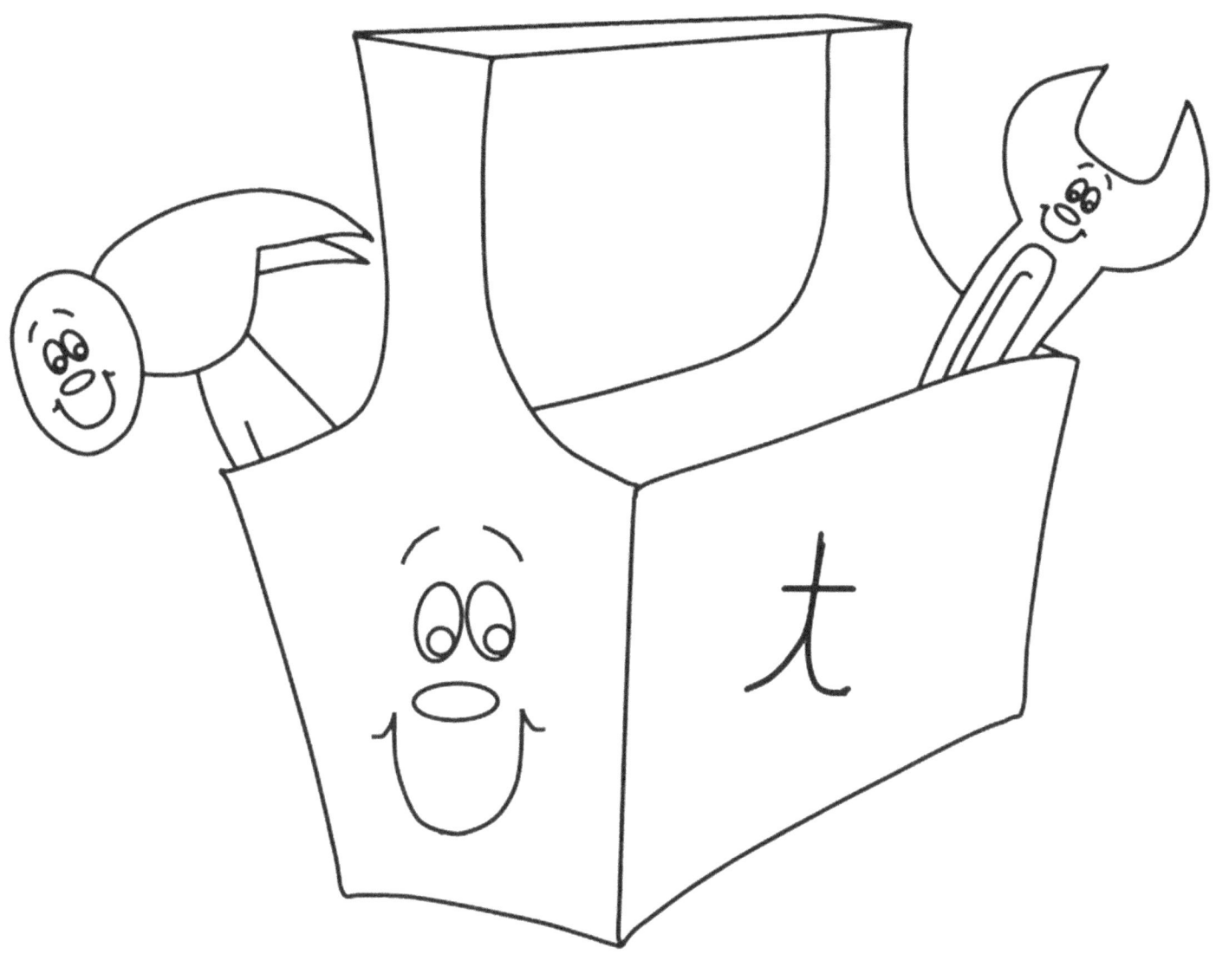

Trace the steps for making the letter t on the following line.

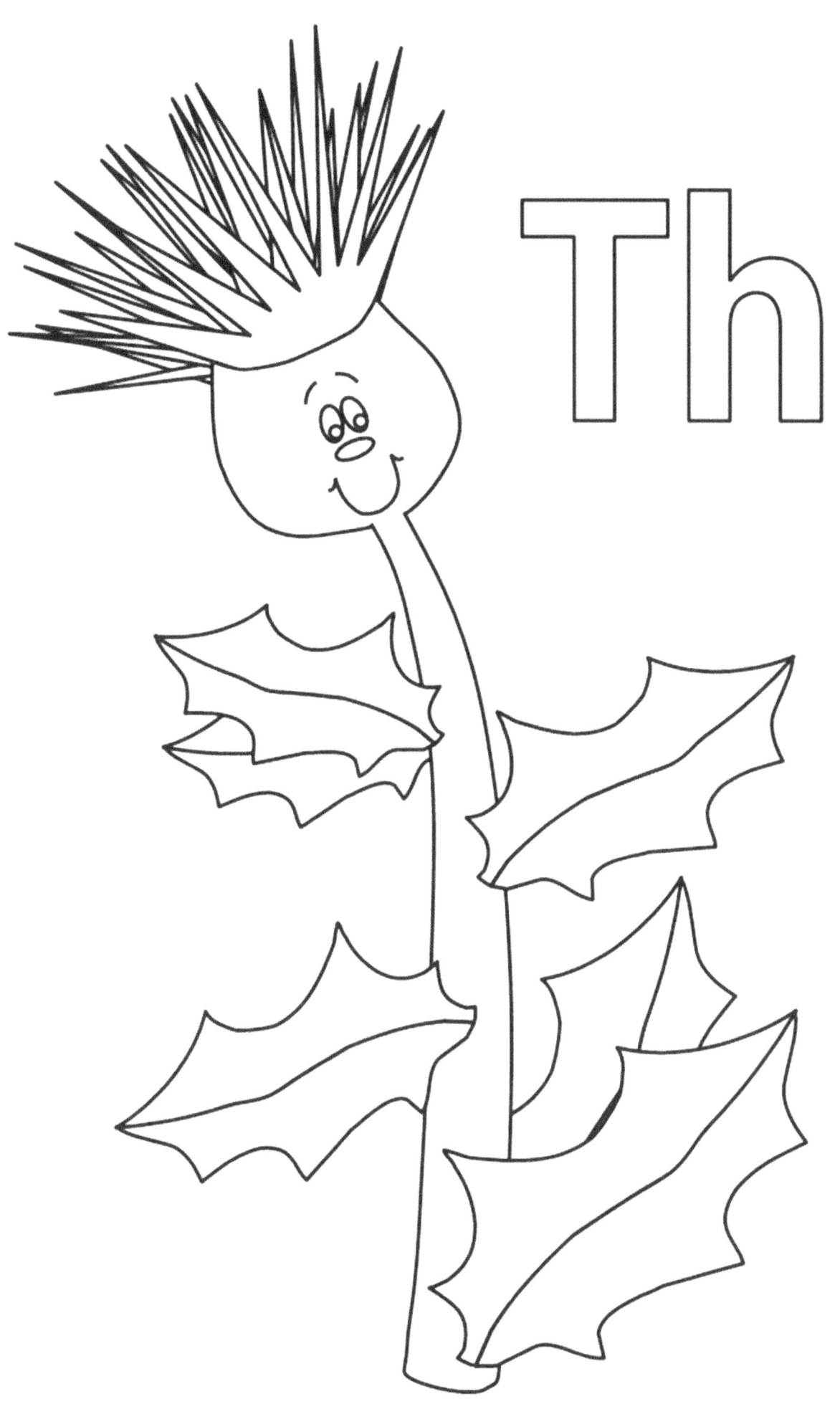

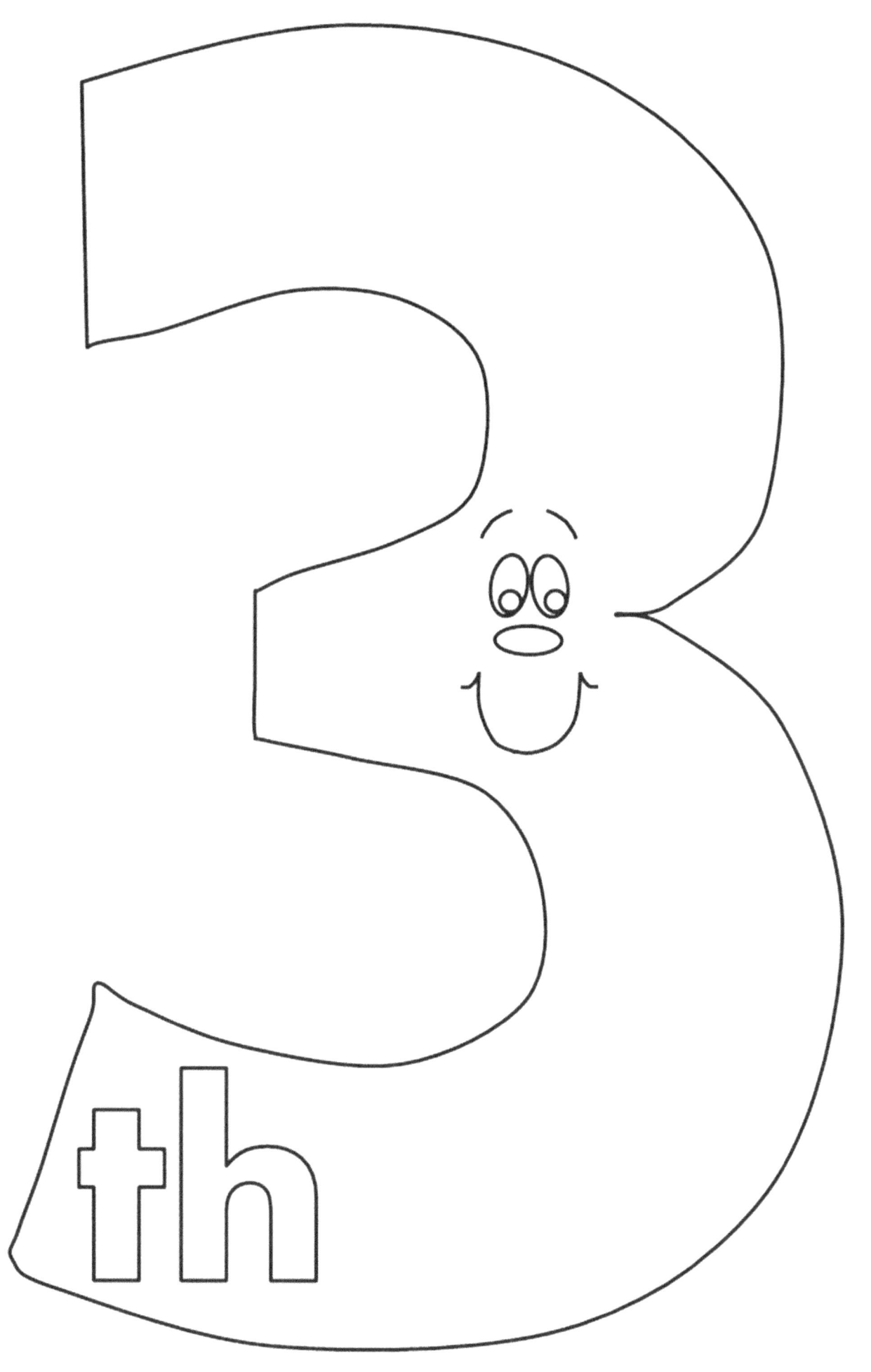

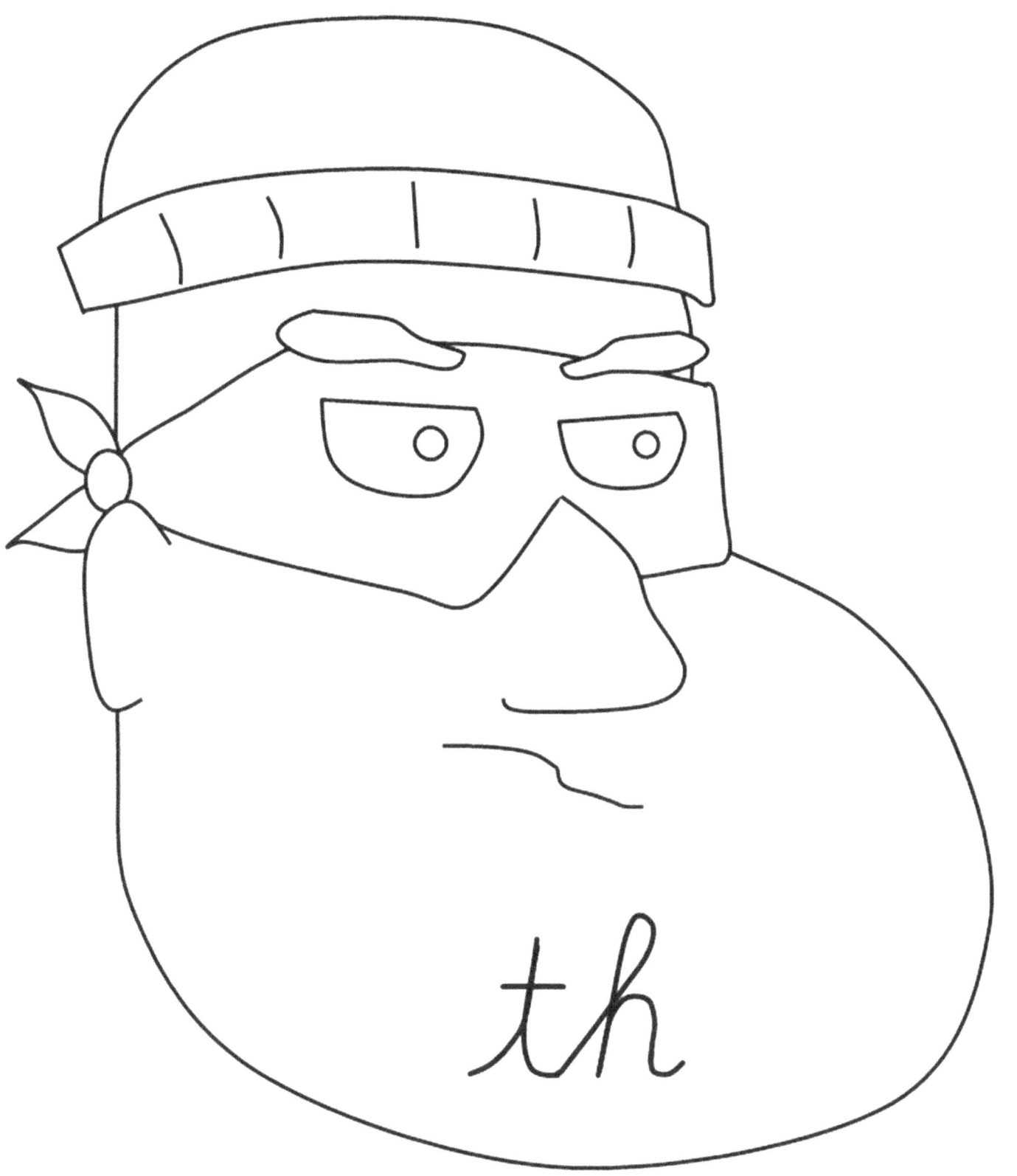

Trace the steps for making the letter th on the following line.

th   th   th   th   th

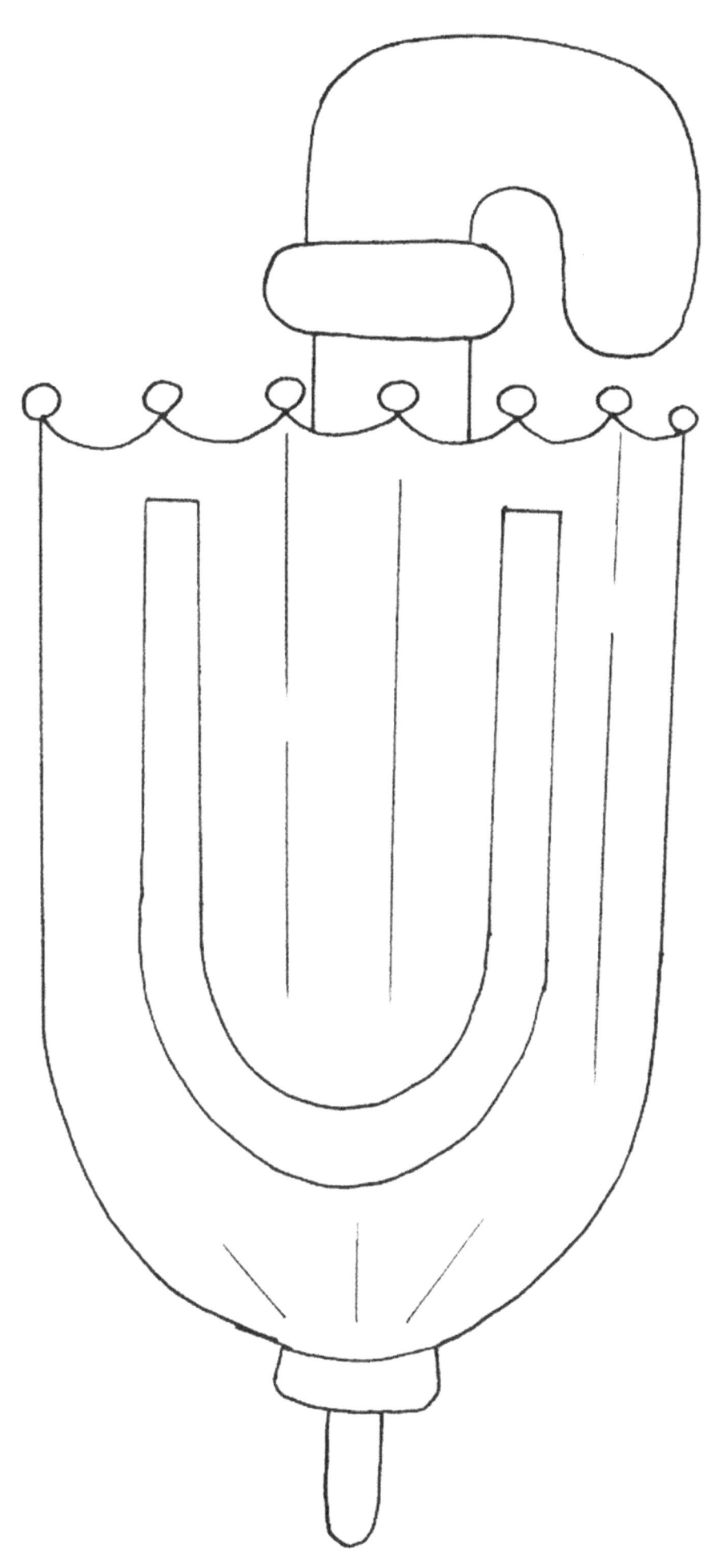

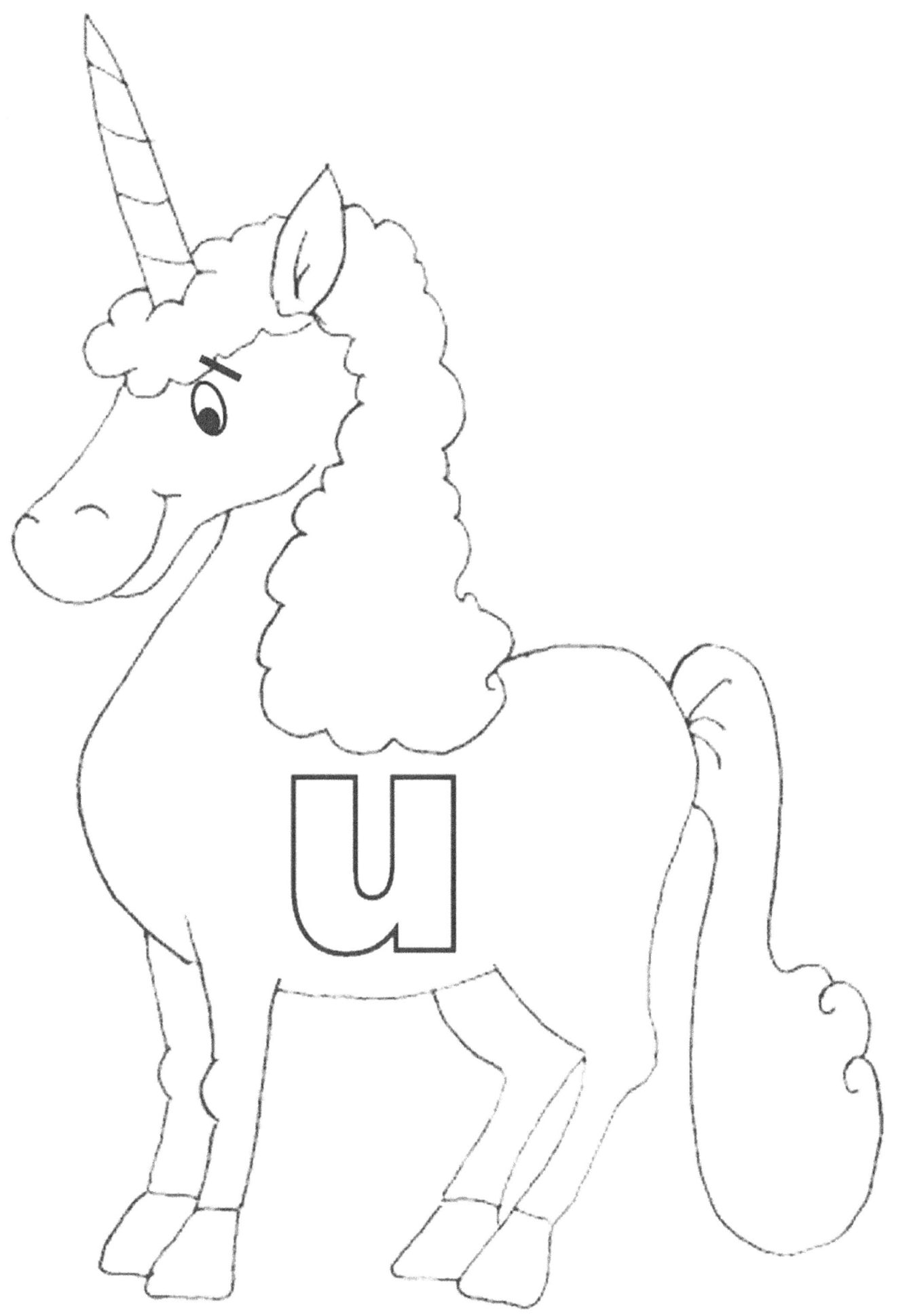

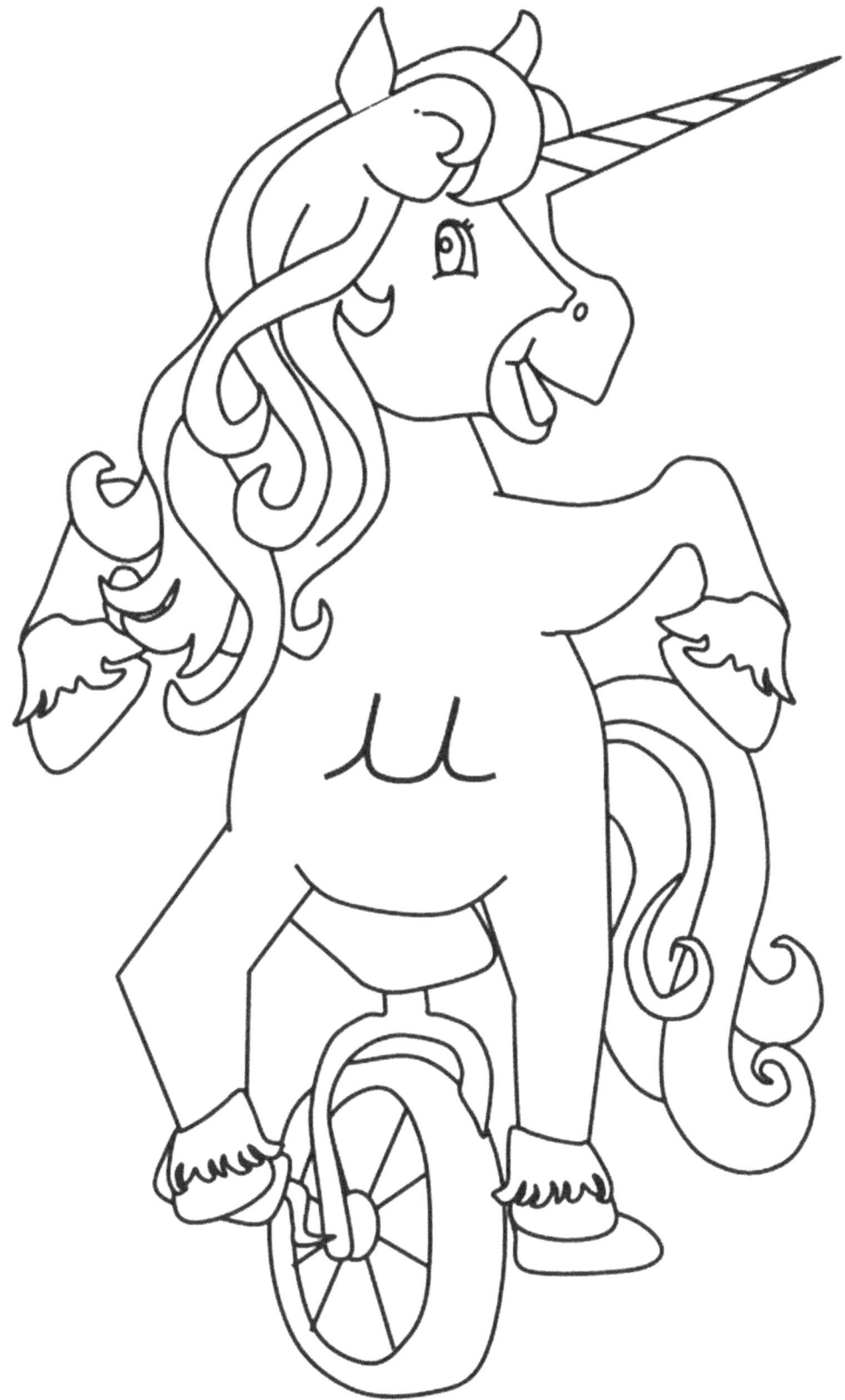

Trace the steps for making the letter u on the following line.

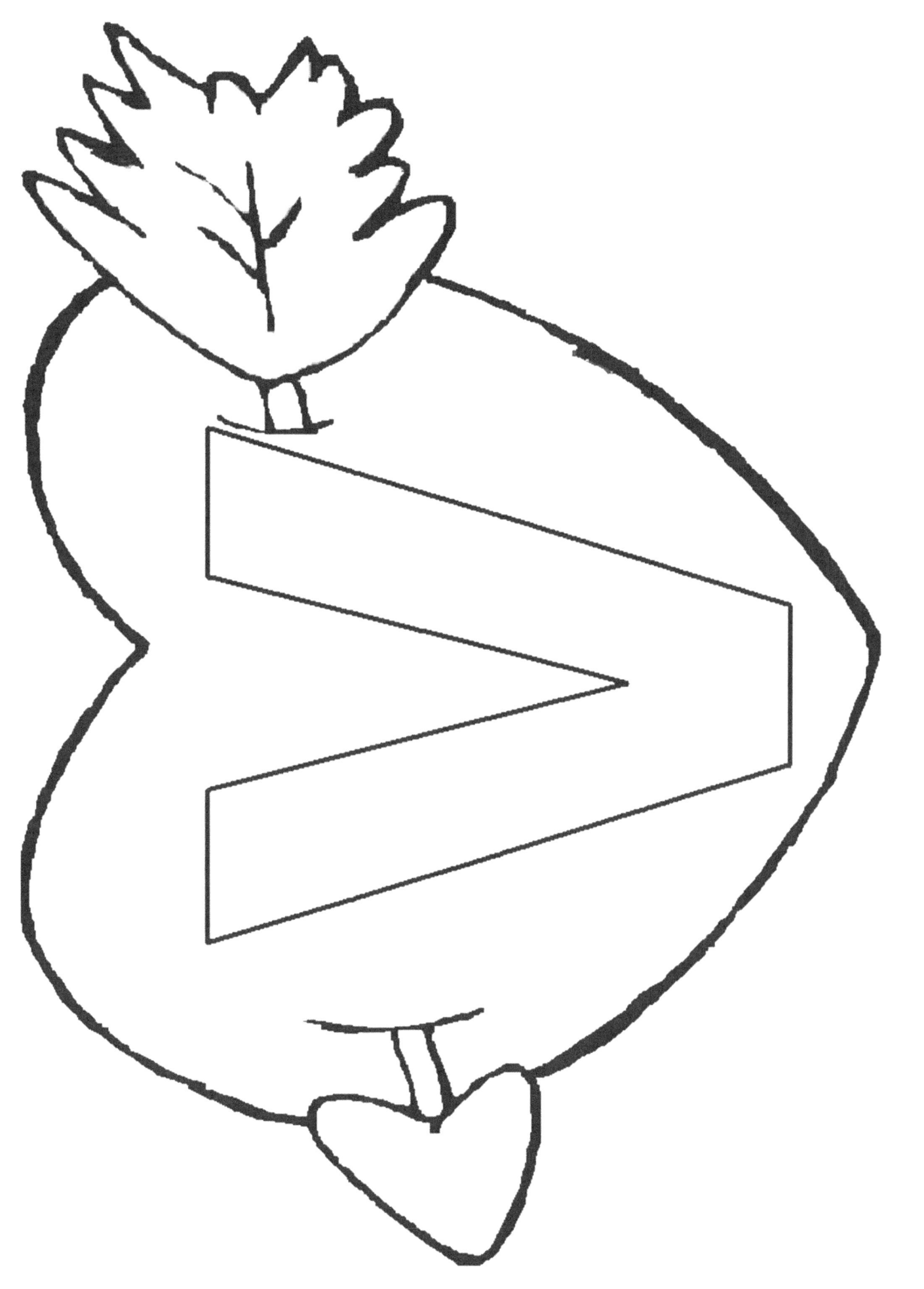

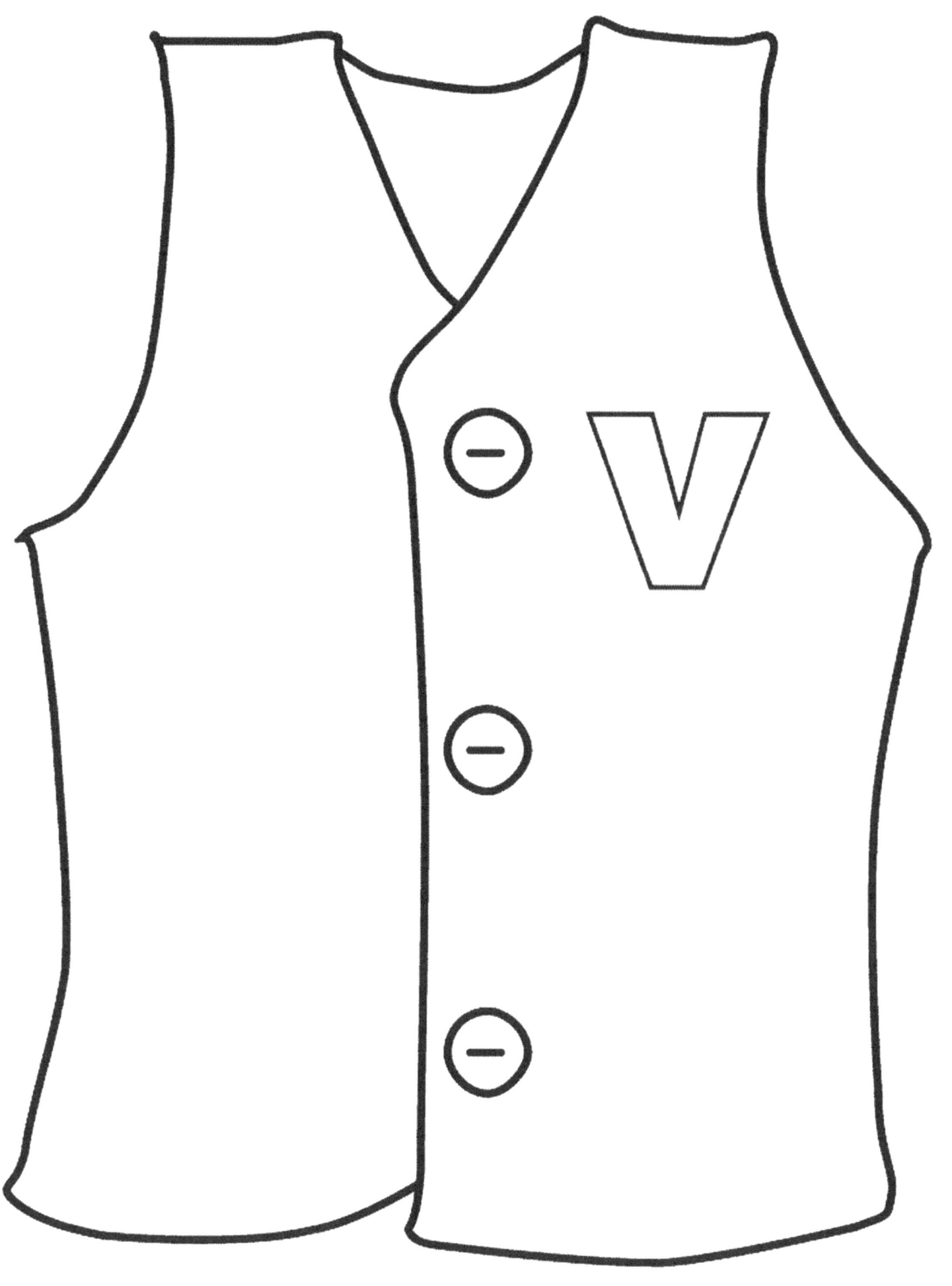

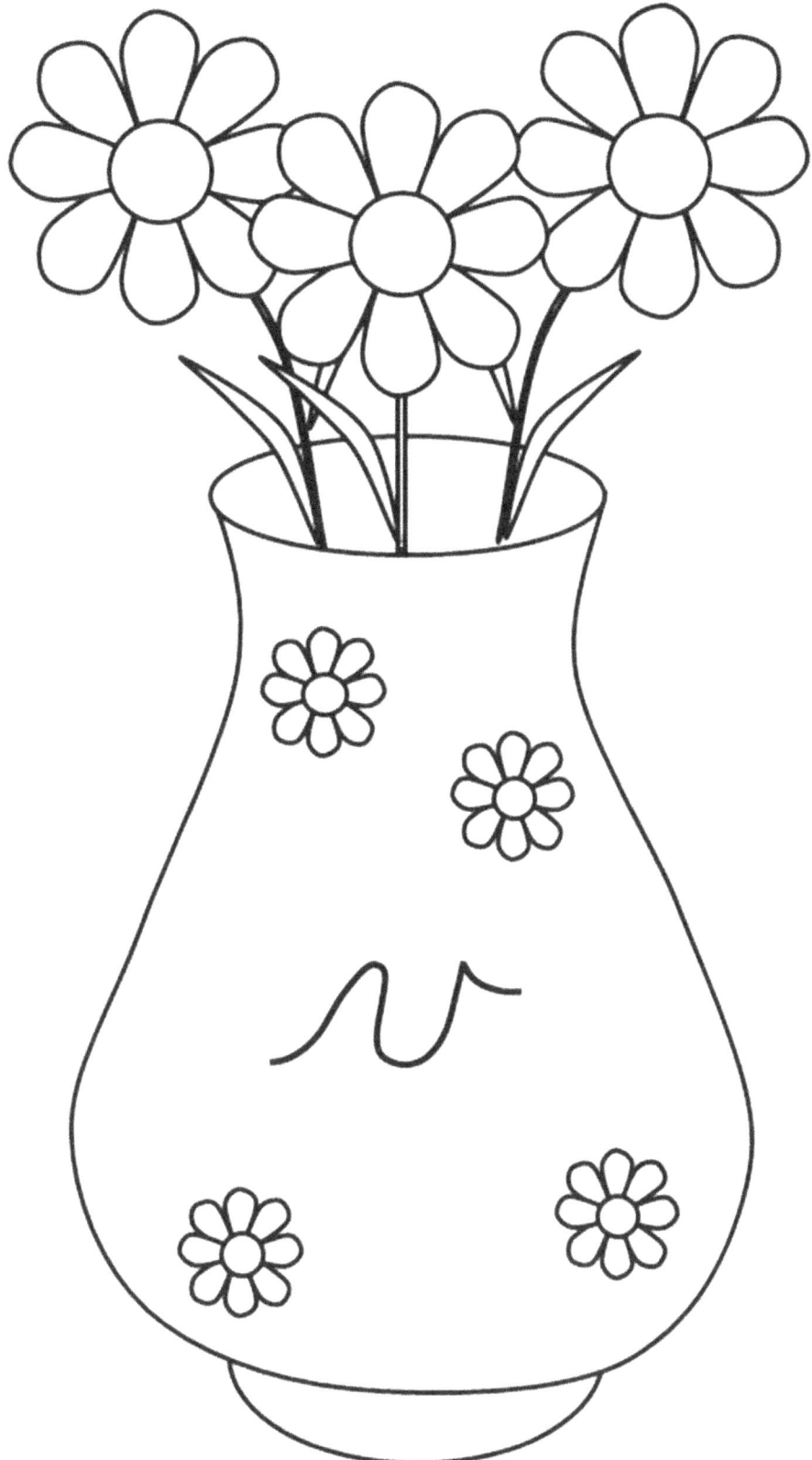

Trace the steps for making the letter v on the following line.

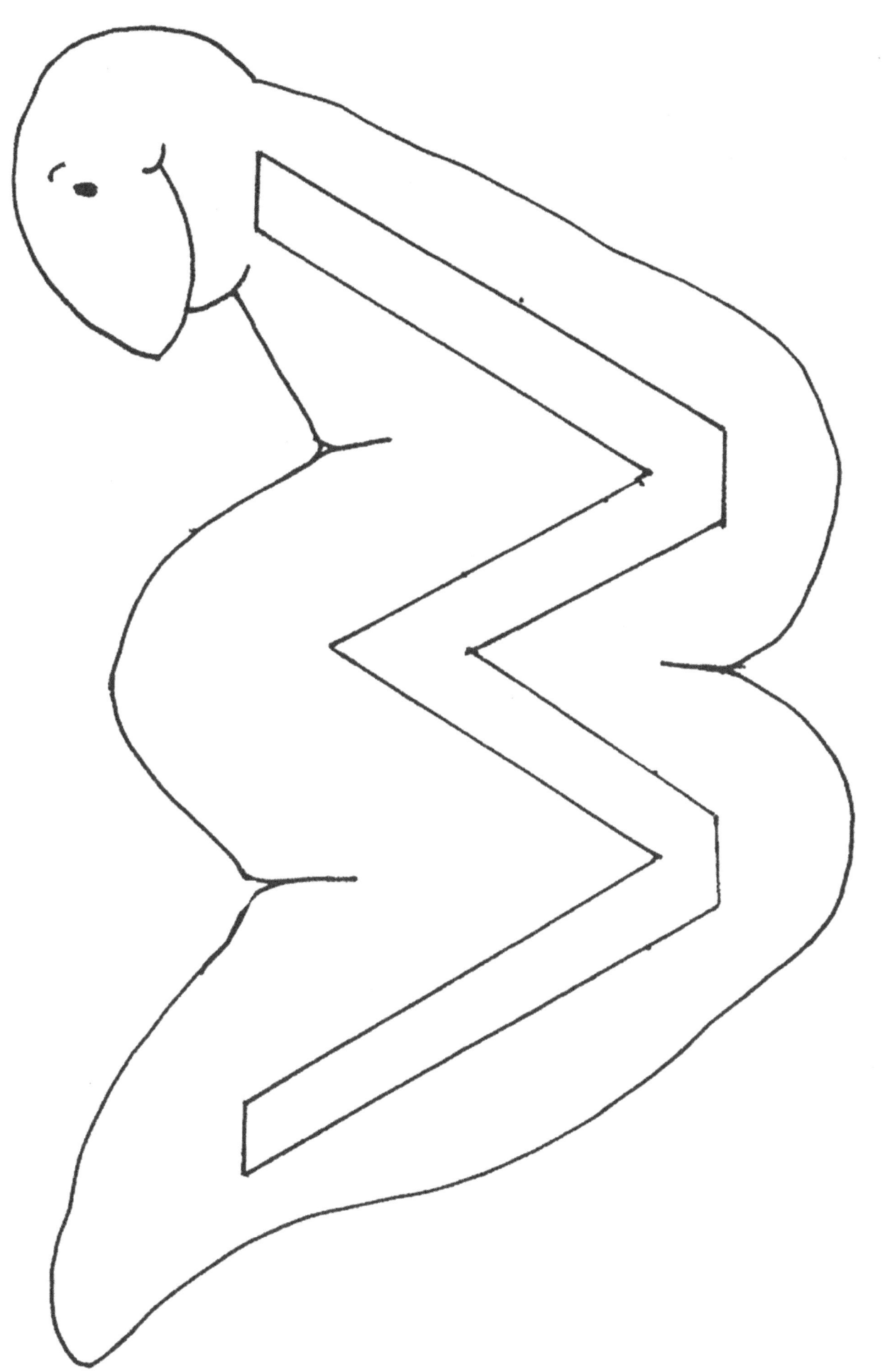

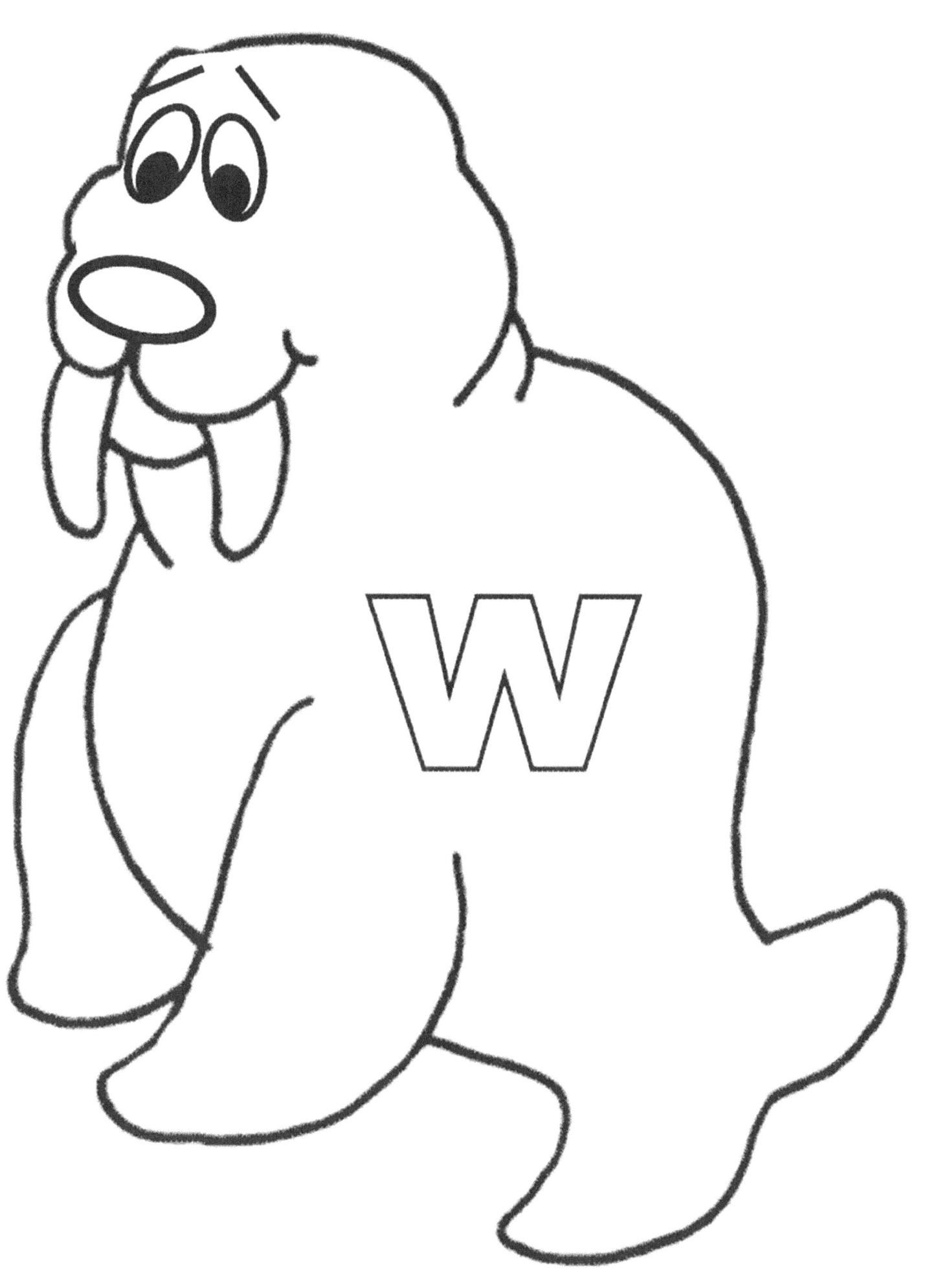

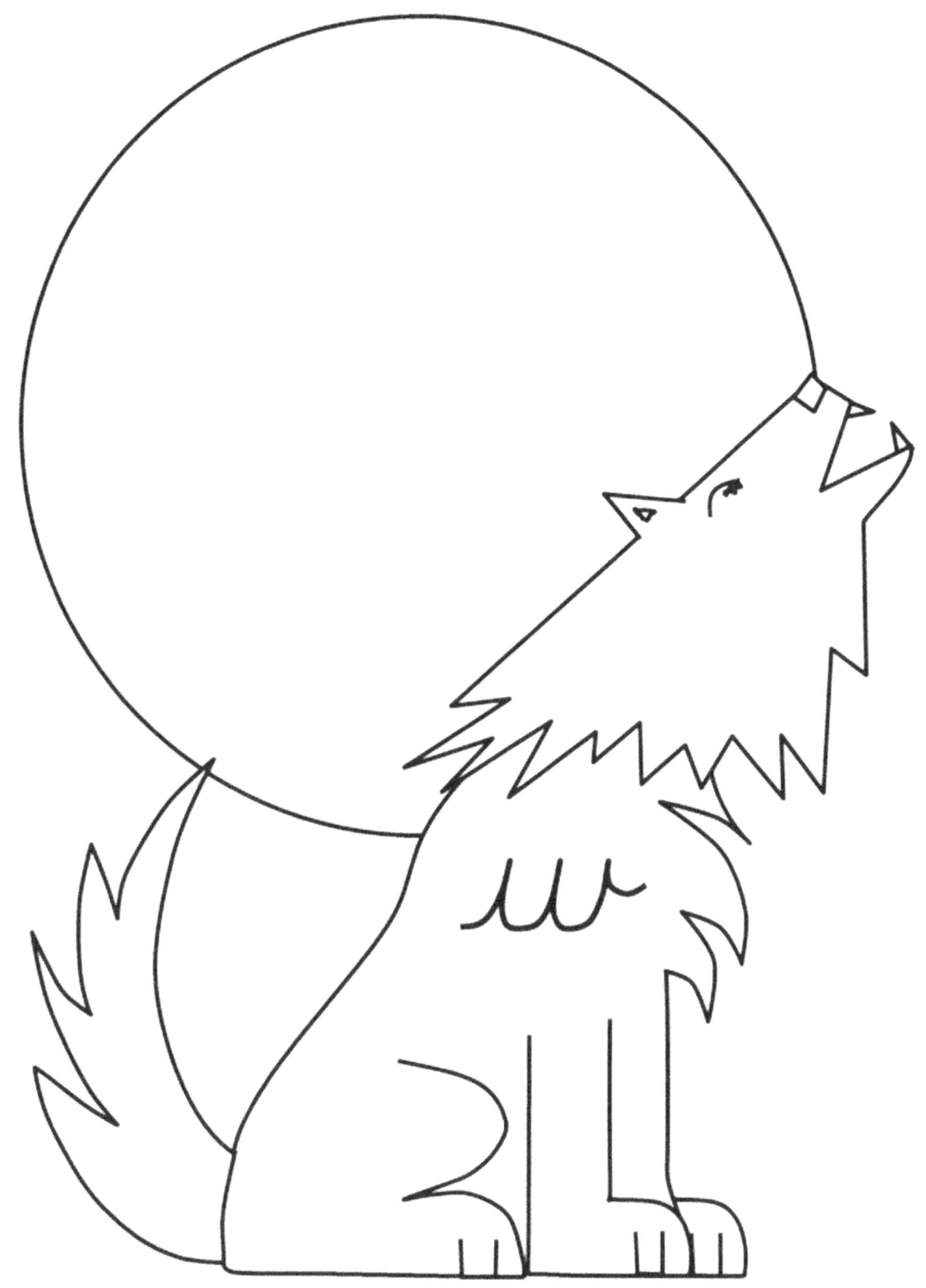

Trace the steps for making the letter w on the following line.

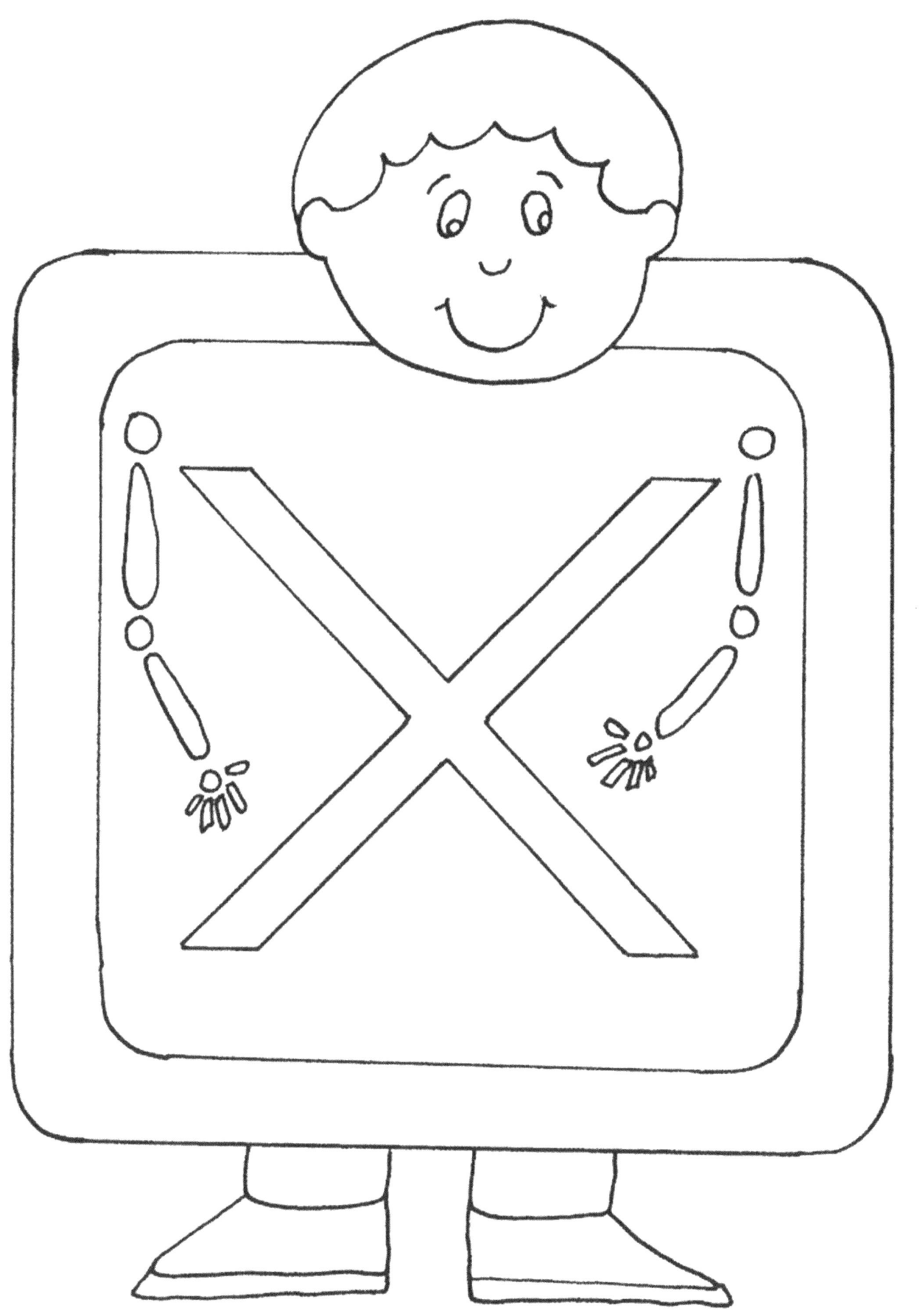

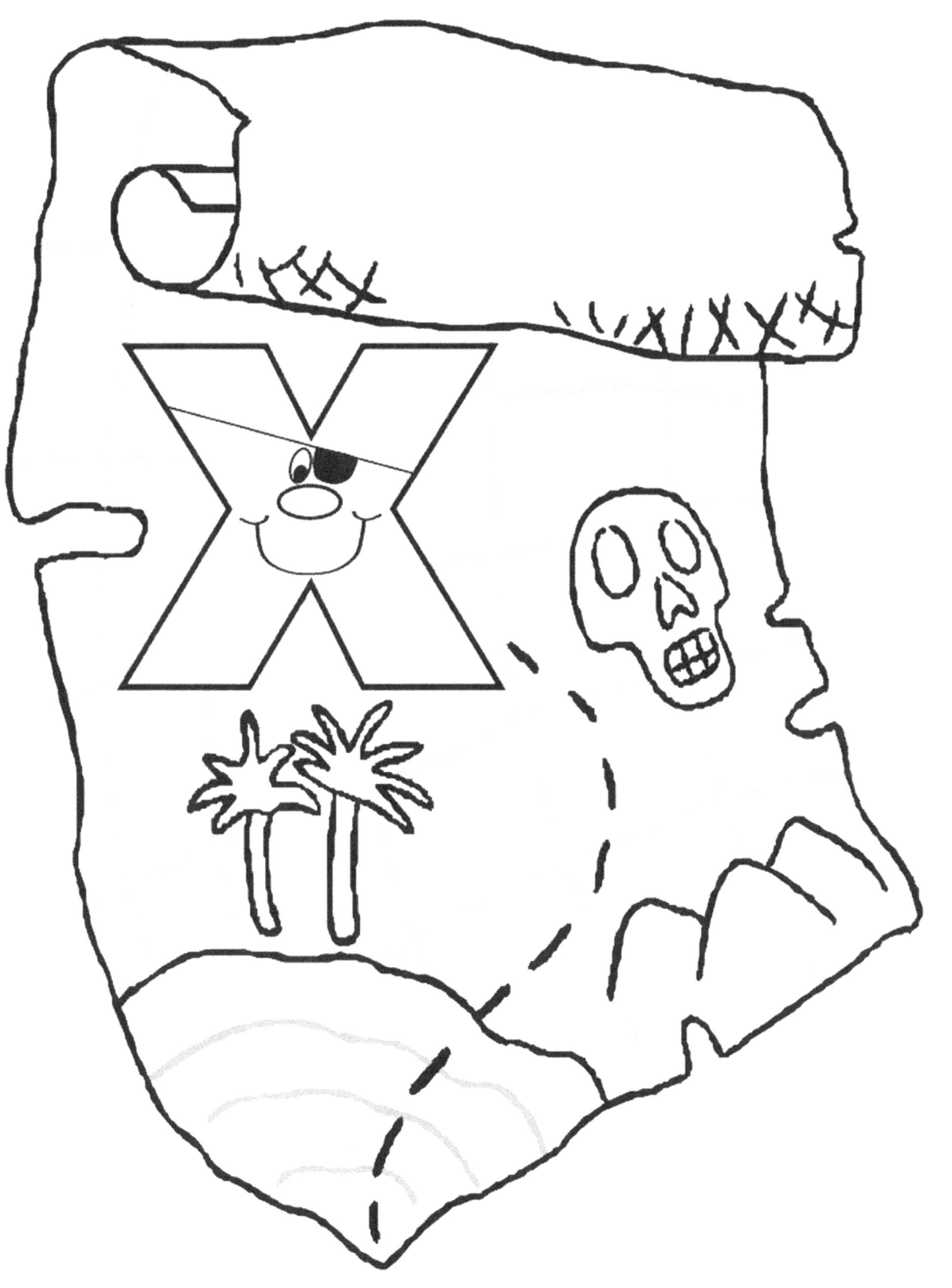

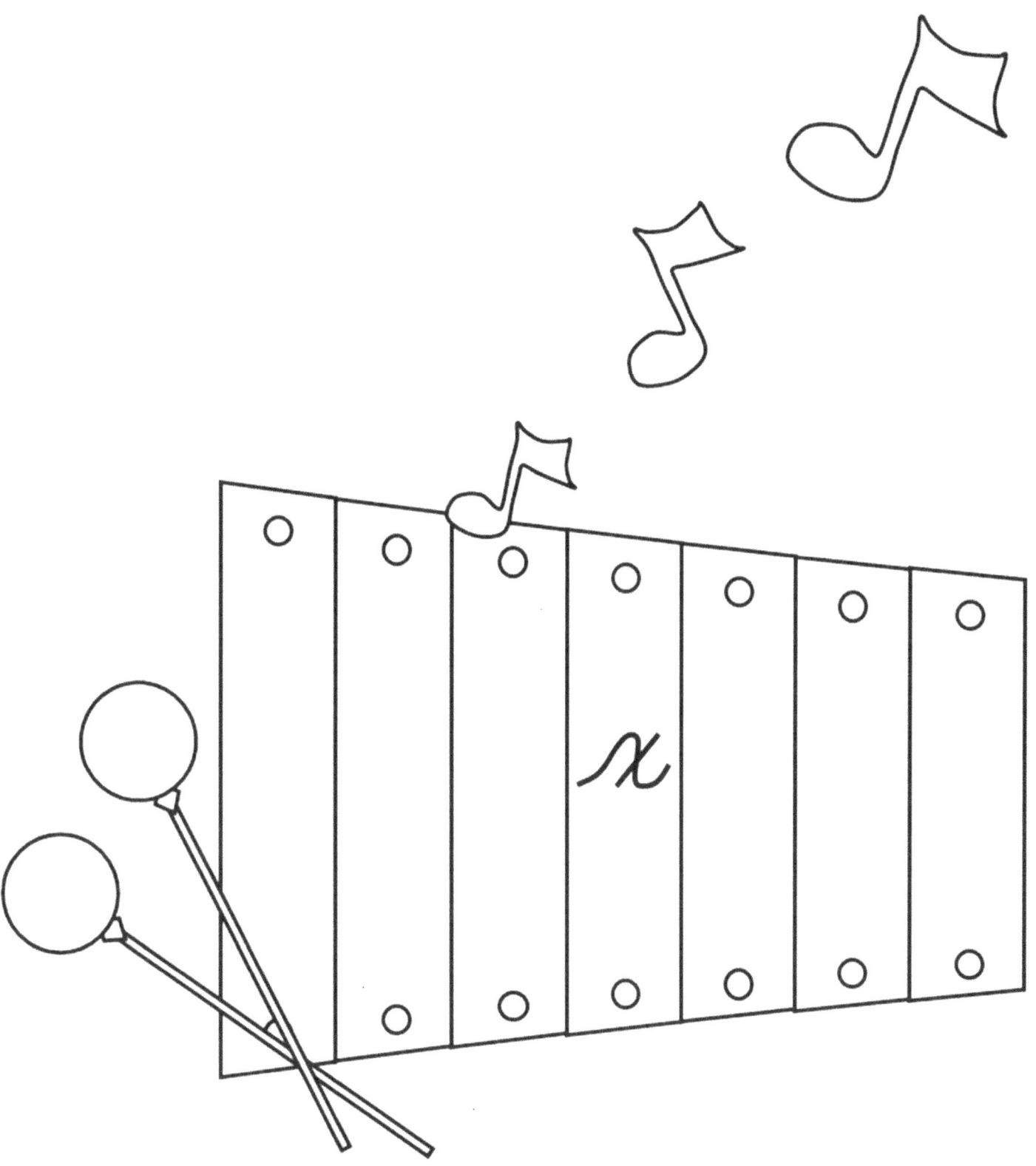

Trace the steps for making the letter x on the following line.

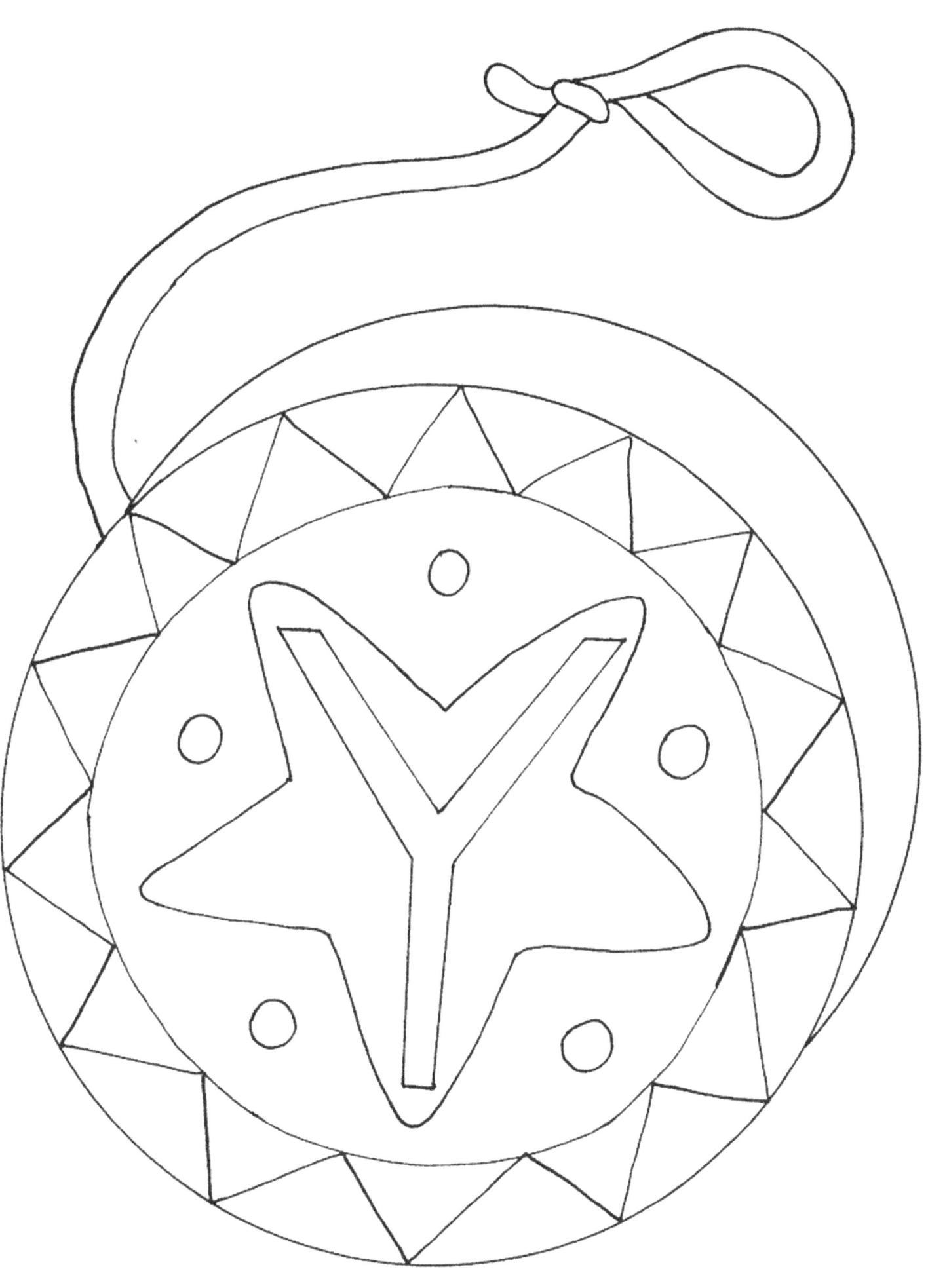

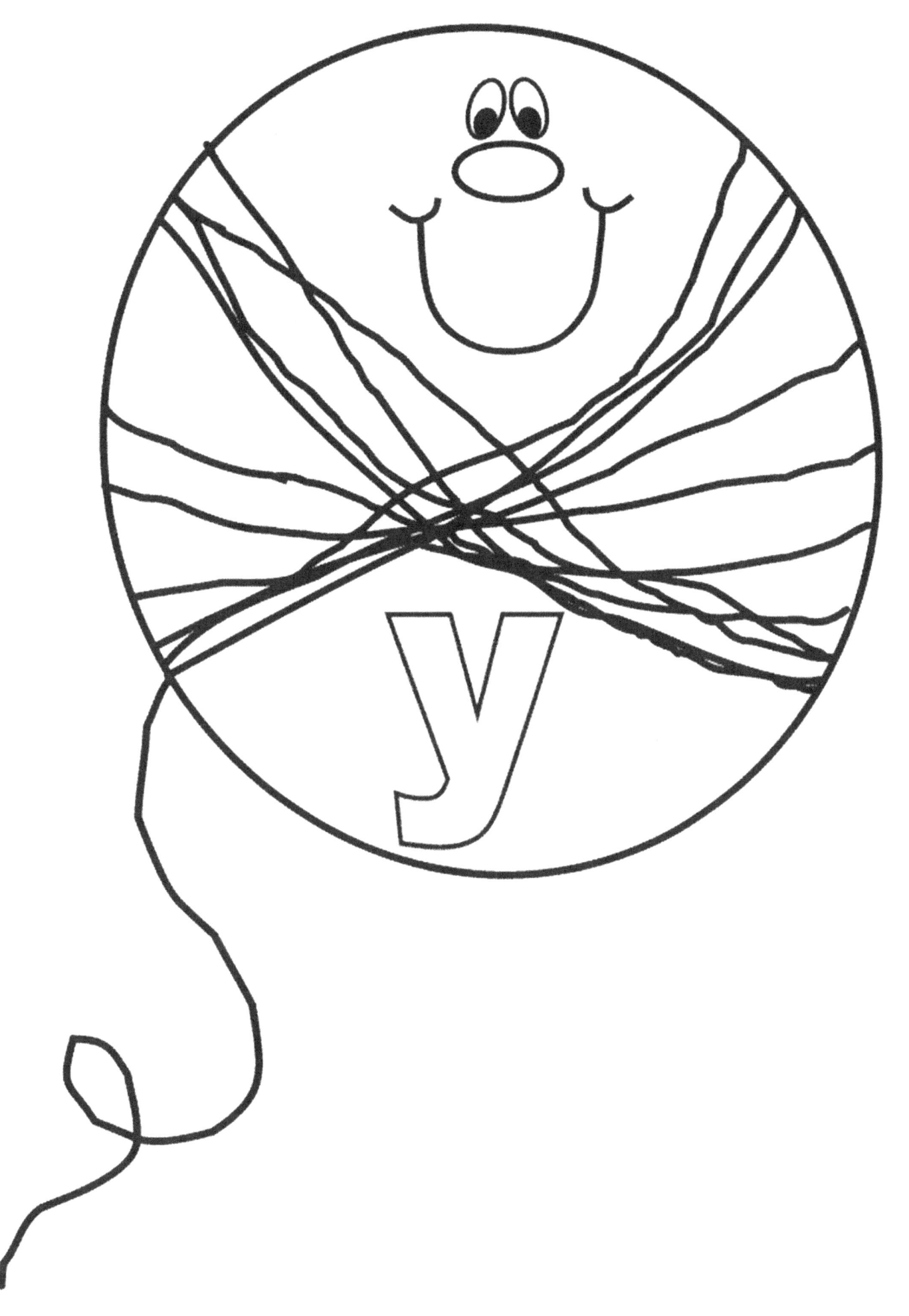

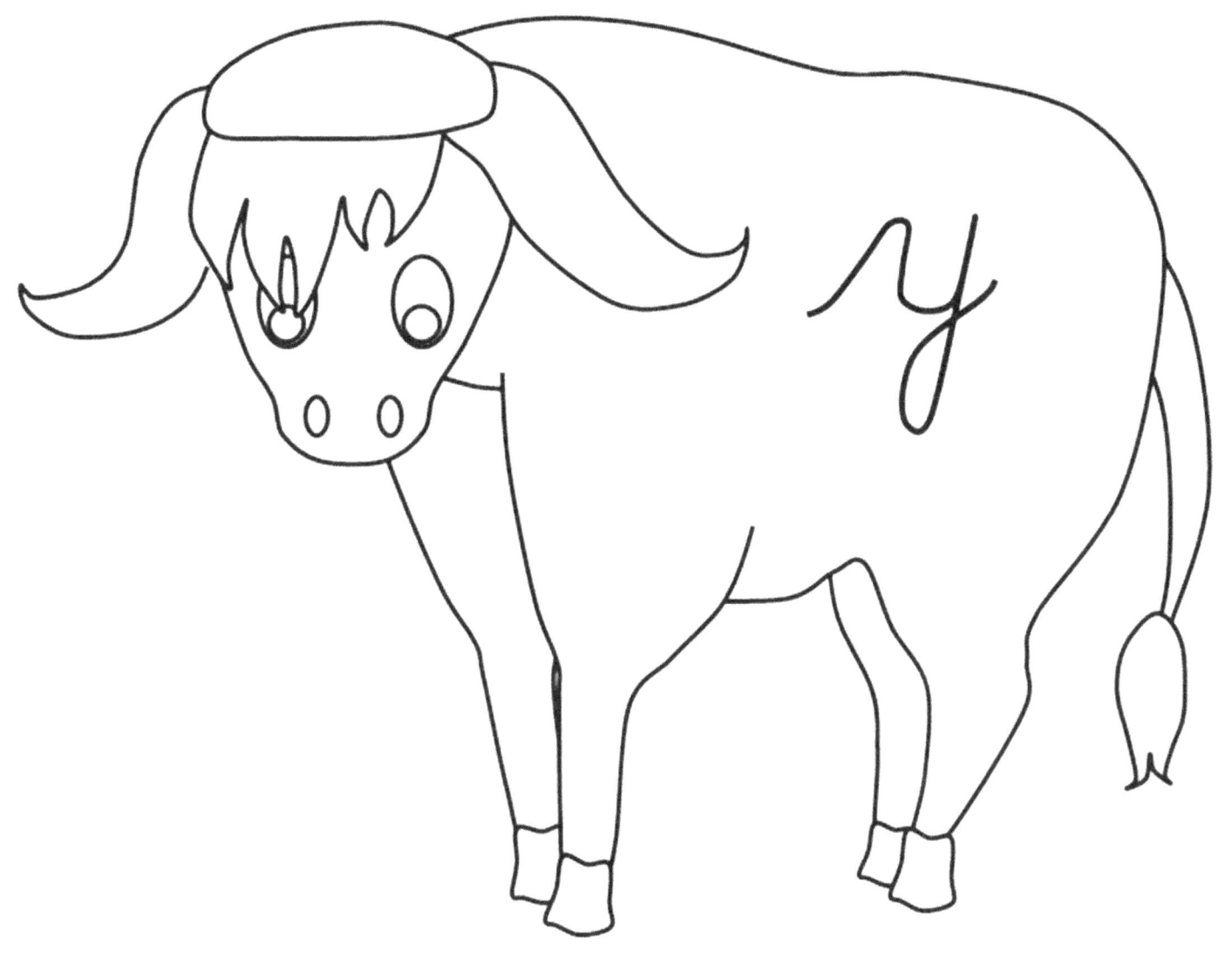

Trace the steps for making the letter y on the following line.

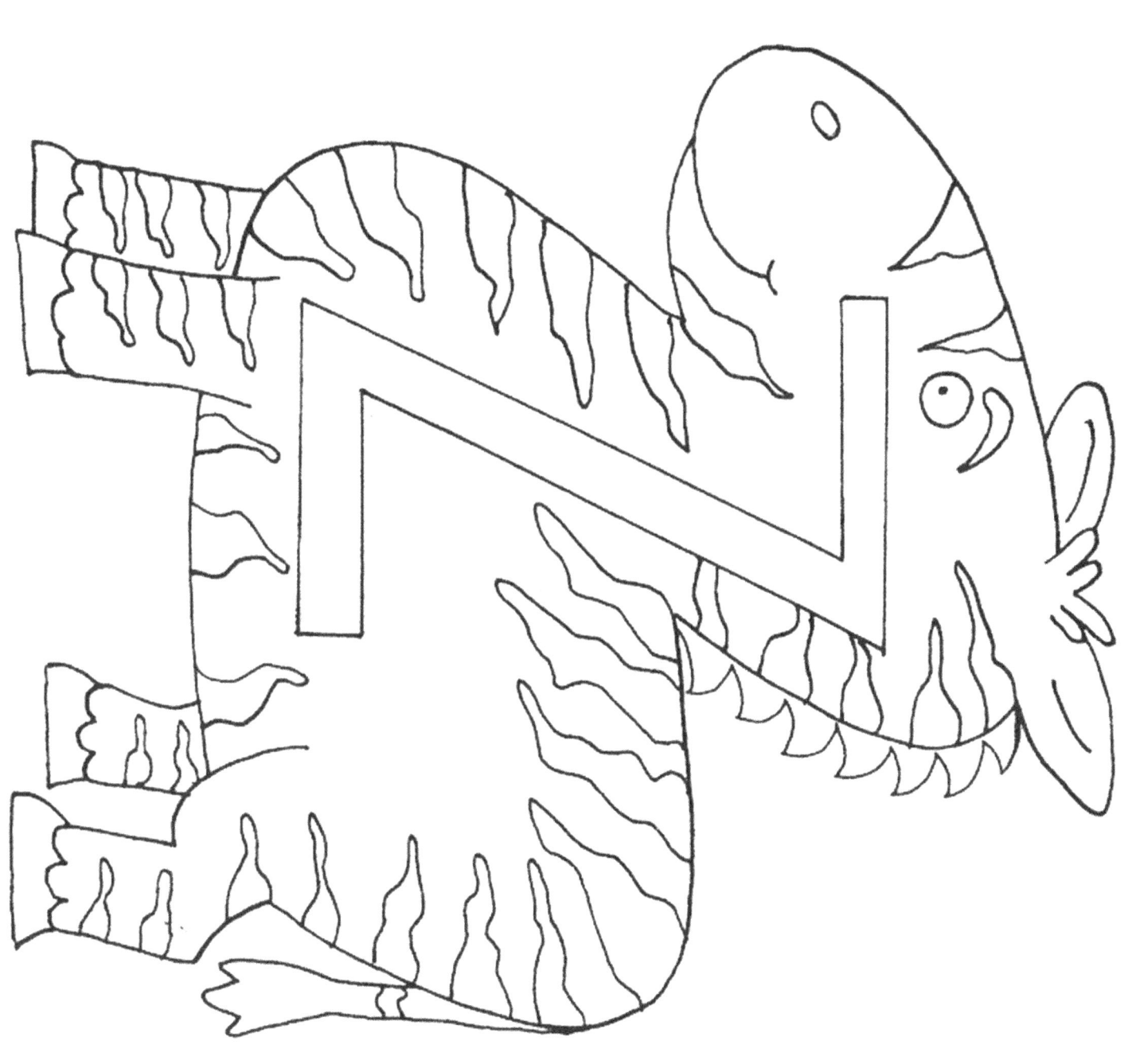

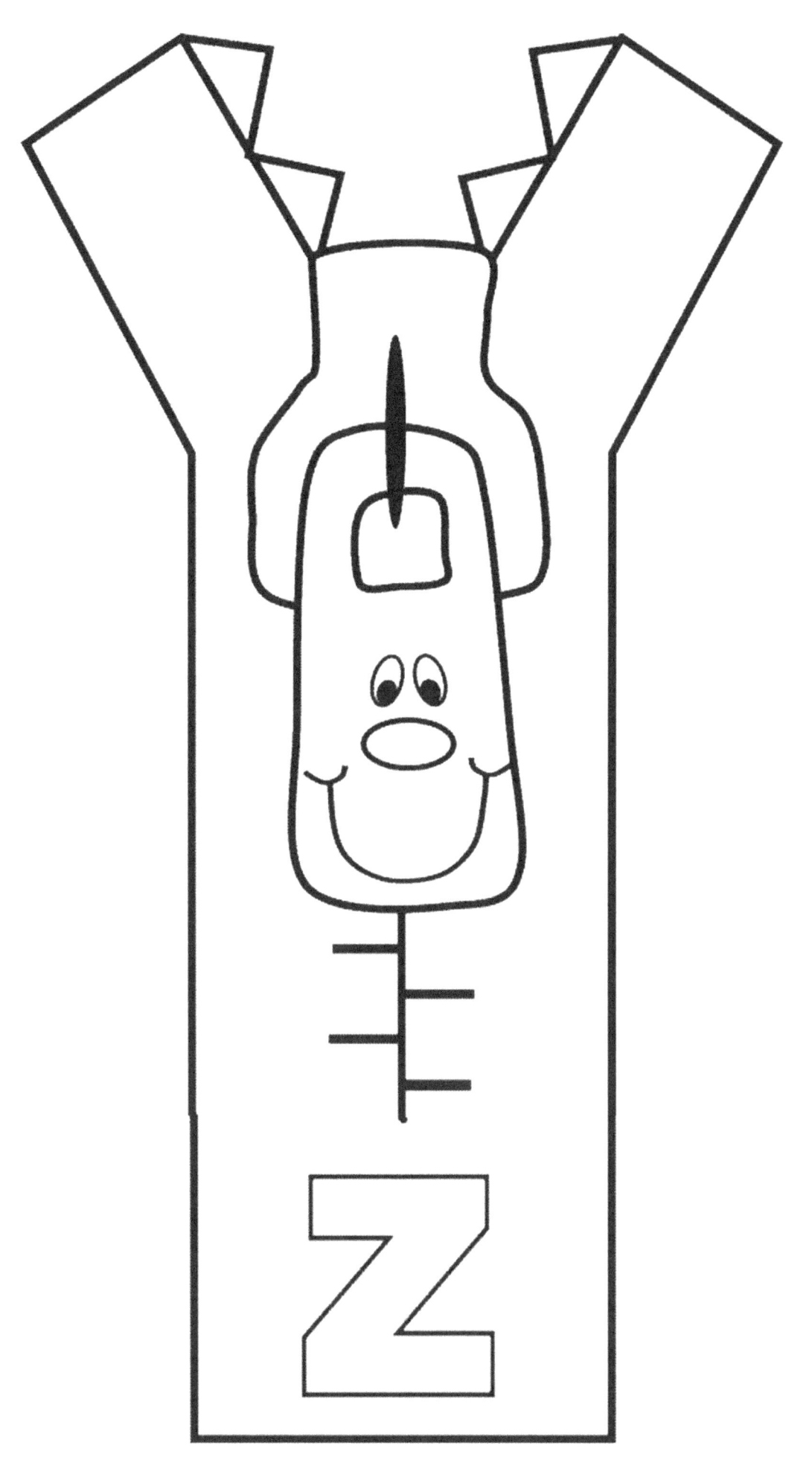

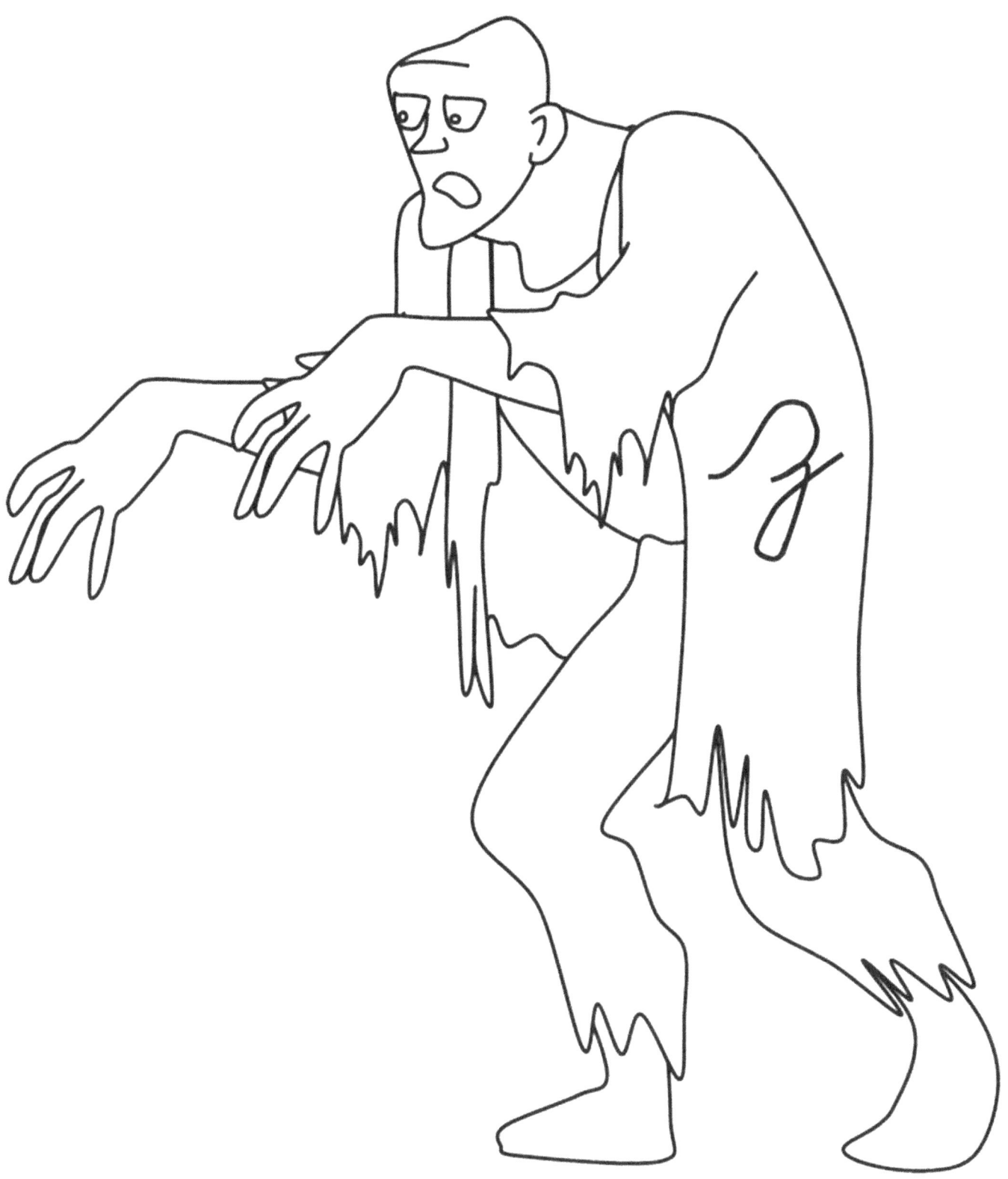

Trace the steps for making the letter z on the following line.

www.ingramcontent.com/pod-product-compliance
Lightning Source LLC
Chambersburg PA
CBHW081511220526
45467CB00010B/2875